# Outstanding African Americans of Congress

by

Shirley Washington, Ph.D.

on a grant from
The United States Capitol Historical Society
200 Maryland Avenue, N.E.
Washington, D.C. 20002

OUTSTANDING
MEMBERS OF
CONGRESS
SERIES
UNITED STATES
CAPITOL
HISTORICAL
SOCIETY

OUTSTANDING AFRICAN AMERICANS OF CONGRESS
Advisory Committee

Russell Adams
Richard A. Baker
Walter Beach
Julian Bond
Charles Harris
Matthew Holden
Benjamin Hooks
Hanes Walton, Jr.

Publication of this book was made possible in part by
generous grants from:

Merrill Lynch & Co. Foundation, Inc.
The Marjorie Merriweather Post Foundation
Time Warner Inc.
The Goodyear Tire & Rubber Company
The Procter & Gamble Company

A special note of appreciation is due to Toni Fay, Vice President, Community Relations,
Time Warner Inc., and to Karen A. McRae on behalf of the Business Policy Review Council
(BPRC) for their generous donations of time and talent in fundraising for this project.

Library of Congress Catalog Card Number: 98-61369
ISBN 0-916200-23-x

Design by Pat Taylor, Inc.
Printed by McArdle Printing Company, Inc.

OUTSTANDING MEMBERS OF CONGRESS SERIES
*Outstanding Women Members of Congress (1995)*
*Outstanding Athletes of Congress (1997)*
*Outstanding African Americans of Congress (1998)*
*Outstanding Environmentalists of Congress (forthcoming)*

(Courtesy of Andrew Young)

*Young was a "hands-on" mayor of Atlanta, always accessible to his constituents.*

His instant rapport with Third World ambassadors made some European nations uneasy, probably due to Young's obvious support for an end to the last vestiges of colonialism.

The guerilla war in Rhodesia, a former British colony, tested the UN's peacekeeping abilities. In fact, the whole Southern tier of the African continent was in turmoil which had East-West Cold War implications as well as racial overtones. Ambassador Young's greatest achievement was pushing the Lancaster House negotiated settlement of the Rhodesian crisis.

Ambassador Young and President Carter took unconventional approaches to foreign policy. Young's honest outspokenness was controversial; yet, it would have been unlikely that an American President from the Deep South could have gained as much credibility for his human rights policy without such a reputable former civil rights preacher as his spokesman.

Young fully expected to hold his post for the duration of the Carter administration. He had consistent backing from his chief; however, his tenure was cut short on August 16, 1979. An unauthorized meeting with the Palestinian Liberation Organization's UN observer led to his removal by President Carter. Although many of his constituents protested, Young regarded it as a liberating experience and held no bitterness nor regret. In fact, he believed that as a private citizen he could be of more use to President Carter as an advisor on human rights and an expert on African affairs.

**His Honor the Mayor**

Ambassador Young, his wife and their four children eagerly returned to Atlanta where he pursued his "Young Ideas," a venture that tried to link his liberal civil rights views and experience with the vast resources of the growing African-American middle class to influence foreign and domestic policy. Traditionally, nations' foreign policies had been made by the societal elite. Young believed in an open foreign policy more responsive to the needs and wishes of all citizens.

Political office attracted him again, however. Maynard Jackson, the first African-American mayor of Atlanta could not succeed himself after two terms. Young ran for the office to bring his city to the attention of the world. He was elected in October 1981 and assumed office on January 4, 1982; he was reelected to a second term in 1985.

As mayor, Andrew Young brought all of his talents to bear to make Atlanta a city of light, tolerance and a thriving metropolis—he called it "a city too busy to hate." Building on the experiences and accomplishments of his African-American predecessor, Young helped Atlanta become a shining example of social integration and economic progress. "My job," he said, "is to see that whites get some of the power and blacks get some of the money." By the end of his eight years in office, he could point to several major accomplishments—a building boom, an expanded airport, set asides for minority-owned businesses and over 70 billion dollars in new investment attracted to the city. Following his terms as mayor and an unsuccessful bid for the Democratic gubernatorial nomination in 1990, Young joined the Law Companies Group, Inc., an engineering and environmental company.

Atlantans attribute Young's international standing for bringing the 1996 Olympics to their city. He worked full-time as co-chairman of the

Board of Directors for the 1996 Summer Olympic Committee in Atlanta. He also served on numerous boards, including the Howard University Board of Trustees, the Georgia Tech Advisory Board, the Board of Directors for the Martin Luther King Center, the Global Infrastructure Fund and the Center for Global Partnership. He has received many awards, most notably the Presidential Medal of Freedom, the nation's highest civilian honor, and more than 35 honorary degrees.

His beloved wife, Jean, died on September 16, 1994, following a long battle with cancer. Soon thereafter, President Bill Clinton took the opportunity of the state visit of South African President Nelson Mandela to announce the naming of Young as chairman of the board of the Southern African Enterprise Development Fund.

Andrew J. Young is a genuine American success story. President Jimmy Carter once called him the greatest public servant he had ever known. Of all his accomplishments as a minister, civil rights leader, politician and diplomat, the most dramatic in terms of symbolism was his service as Ambassador to the United Nations. As an African American representing the most powerful nation in the world, Young enhanced America's moral standing as a nation devoted to human rights for all the peoples of the world.

**For Further Reading:**

William L. Clay, *Just Permanent Interests: Black Americans in Congress, 1870-1992*, (1993).
Carl Gardner, *Andrew Young: A Biography*, (1978).
Andrew Young, *A Way Out of No Way: The Spiritual Memoirs of Andrew Young*, (1994).
Andrew Young, "The United States and Africa: Victory for Diplomacy," *Foreign Affairs* (1981).

# African-American Members of Congress, 1870-1998: A Chronological Listing

As of July, 1998, 104 African Americans have served in Congress, four in the Senate and one hundred in the House of Representatives.

## Senate

Hiram R. Revels (R-MS), 1870-71
Blanche K. Bruce (R-MS), 1875-81
Edward W. Brooke (R-MA), 1967-79
Carol Moseley-Braun (D-IL), 1993-

## House of Representatives

Joseph H. Rainey (R-SC), 1870-79
Jefferson F. Long (R-GA), 1870-71
Robert B. Elliott (R-SC), 1871-74
Robert C. De Large (R-SC), 1871-73
Benjamin S. Turner (R-AL), 1871-73
Josiah T. Walls (R-FL), 1871-76
Richard H. Cain (R-SC), 1873-75, 1877-79
John R. Lynch (R-MS), 1873-77, 1882-83
James T. Rapier (R-AL), 1873-75
Alonzo J. Ransier (R-SC), 1873-75
Jeremiah Haralson (R-AL) 1875-77
John A. Hyman (R-NC) 1875-77
Charles E. Nash (R-LA) 1875-77
Robert Smalls (R-SC), 1875-79, 1882-83, 1884-87
James E. O'Hara (R-NC), 1883-87
Henry P. Cheatham (R-NC), 1889-93
John M. Langston (R-VA), 1890-91
Thomas E. Miller (R-SC), 1890-91
George W. Murray (R-SC), 1893-95, 1896-97
George H. White (R-NC), 1897-1901
Oscar De Priest (R-IL), 1929-35
Arthur W. Mitchell (D-IL), 1935-43
William L. Dawson (D-IL), 1943-70
Adam Clayton Powell Jr. (D-NY), 1945-67, 1969-71
Charles C. Diggs Jr. (D-MI), 1955-80
Robert N.C. Nix (D-PA), 1958-79
Augustus F. Hawkins (D-CA), 1963-91
John Conyers Jr. (D-MI), 1965-
Louis Stokes (D-OH), 1969-
William L. Clay (D-MO), 1969-
Shirley Chisholm (D-NY), 1969-83
George W. Collins (D-IL), 1970-72
Ronald V. Dellums (D-CA), 1971-98
Walter E. Fauntroy (D-DC), 1971-91
Ralph H. Metcalfe (D-IL), 1971-78
Parren J. Mitchell (D-MD), 1971-87
Charles B. Rangel (D-NY), 1971-
Yvonne B. Burke (D-CA), 1973-79
Cardiss Collins (D-IL), 1973-97
Barbara C. Jordan (D-TX), 1973-79
Andrew Young (D-GA), 1973-77
Harold E. Ford (D-TN), 1975-97

Julian C. Dixon (D-CA), 1979-
Melvyn H. Evans (R-VI), 1979-81
William H. Gray III (D-PA), 1979-91
George T. "Mickey" Leland (D-TX), 1979-89
Bennett McVey Stewart (D-IL), 1979-81
George W. Crockett Jr. (D-MI), 1981-91
Mervyn M. Dymally (D-CA), 1981-93
Gus Savage (D-IL), 1981-93
Harold D. Washington (D-IL), 1981-83
Katie B. Hall (D-IN), 1983-85
Charles A. Hayes (D-IL), 1983-93
Major R. Owens (D-NY), 1983-
Edolphus Towns (D-NY), 1983-
Alan D. Wheat (D-MO), 1983-95
Alton Waldon Jr. (D-NY), 1986-87
Mike Espy (D-MS), 1987-93
Floyd H. Flake (D-NY), 1987-97
John Lewis (D-GA), 1987-
Kweisi Mfume (D-MD), 1987-96
Donald M. Payne (D-NJ), 1989-
Craig Washington (D-TX), 1989-95
Lucien Blackwell (D-PA), 1991-95
Barbara-Rose Collins (D-MI), 1991-97
Gary Franks (R-CT), 1991-97
William Jefferson (D-LA), 1991-
Eleanor Holmes Norton (D-DC), 1991-
Maxine Waters (D-CA), 1991-
Eva Clayton (D-NC), 1992-
Sanford Bishop (D-GA), 1993-
Corrinne Brown (D-FL), 1993-
James E. Clyburn (D-SC), 1993-
Cleo Fields (D-LA), 1993-97
Alcee Hastings (D-FL), 1993-
Earl Hilliard (D-AL), 1993-
Eddie Bernice Johnson (D-TX), 1993-
Cynthia McKinney (D-GA), 1993-
Carrie Meek (D-FL), 1993-
Mel Reynolds (D-IL), 1993-96
Bobby Rush (D-IL), 1993-
Robert Scott (D-VA), 1993-
Bennie Thompson (D-MS), 1993-
Walter Tucker (D-CA), 1993-97
Melvin Watt (D-NC), 1993-
Albert Wynn (D-MD), 1993-
Chaka Fattah (D-PA), 1995-
Victor Frazer (I-VI), 1995-97
Jesse Jackson, Jr. (D-IL), 1995-
Sheila Jackson Lee (D-TX), 1995-

*(continued on next page)*

J.C. Watts (R-OK), 1995-
Elijah E. Cummings (D-MD), 1996-
Juanita Millender-McDonald (D-CA), 1996-
Julia M. Carson (D-IN), 1997-
Donna M. Christian-Green (D-VI), 1997-
Danny Davis (D-IL), 1997-
Harold E. Ford, Jr. (D-TN), 1997-
Carolyn C. Kilpatrick (D-MI), 1997-
Meeks, Gregory W. (D-NY), 1998-
Lee, Barbara (D-CA), 1998-

Sources: *Black Americans in Congress, 1917-1989*, (GPO, 1990); Mildred Amer, *Black Members of the United States Congress, 1789-1993*, (CRS Report 93-671 GOV, 20 July 1993); *Members of Congress Since 1789* (Congressional Quarterly, Inc., 1985); *Congressional Directory* for the 104th Congress, (GPO, 1995); *Congressional Yellow Book* (Spring and Summer, 1998).

# African-American Members of Congress, 1870-1998: An Alphabetical Listing

(Senators in italics)

Bishop, Sanford (D-GA), 1993-
Blackwell, Lucien (D-PA), 1991-95
*Brooke, Edward W. (R-MA), 1967-79*
Brown, Corrinne (D-FL), 1993-
*Bruce, Blanche K. (R-MS), 1875-81*
Burke, Yvonne B. (D-CA), 1973-79
Cain, Richard H. (R-SC), 1873-75, 1877-79
Carson, Julia M. (D-IN), 1997-
Cheatham, Henry P. (R-NC), 1889-93
Chisholm, Shirley (D-NY), 1969-83
Christian-Green, Donna M. (D-VI), 1997-
Clay, William L. (D-MO), 1969-
Clayton, Eva (D-NC), 1992-
Clyburn, James E. (D-SC), 1993-
Collins, Barbara-Rose (D-MI), 1991-97
Collins, Cardiss (D-IL) 1973-97
Collins, George W. (D-IL), 1970-72
Conyers, John Jr. (D-MI), 1965-
Crockett, George W. Jr. (D-MI), 1980-91
Cummings, Elijah E. (D-MD), 1996-
Dawson, William L. (D-IL), 1943-70
Davis, Danny (D-IL), 1997-
De Large, Robert C. (R-SC), 1871-73
Dellums, Ronald V. (D-CA), 1971-98
De Priest, Oscar (R-IL), 1929-35
Diggs, Charles C. Jr. (D-MI), 1955-80
Dixon, Julian C. (D-CA), 1979-
Dymally, Mervyn M. (D-CA), 1981-93
Elliott, Robert B. (R-SC), 1871-74
Espy, Mike (D-MS), 1987-93
Evans, Melvyn H. (R-VI), 1979-81
Fattah, Chaka (D-PA), 1995-
Fauntroy, Walter E. (D-DC), 1971-91
Fields, Cleo (D-LA), 1993-97
Flake, Floyd H. (D-NY) 1987-97
Ford, Harold E. (D-TN), 1975-97
Ford, Harold E. Jr. (D-TN), 1997-
Franks, Gary (R-CT), 1991-97
Frazer, Victor (I-VI), 1995-97
Gray, William H., III (D-PA), 1979-91
Hall, Katie B. (D-IN), 1983-85
Haralson, Jeremiah (R-AL), 1875-77
Hastings, Alcee (D-FL), 1993-
Hawkins, Augustus F. (D-CA), 1963-91
Hayes, Charles A. (D-IL), 1983-93
Hilliard, Earl (D-AL), 1993-
Hyman, John A. (R-NC), 1875-77
Jackson, Jesse Jr. (D-IL), 1995-
Jefferson, William (D-LA), 1991-
Johnson, Eddie Bernice (D-TX), 1993-
Jordan, Barbara C. (D-TX), 1973-79
Kilpatrick, Carolyn C. (D-MI), 1997-
Langston, John M. (R-VA), 1890-91

*(continued on next page)*

# Contents

# A NOTE ABOUT THIS SERIES

*O*utstanding African Americans of Congress is the third book in the *Outstanding Members of Congress Series* begun by the United States Capitol Historical Society in 1995 with the publication of *Outstanding Women Members of Congress* and continued in 1997 with the publication of *Outstanding Athletes of Congress*. Like the first two volumes on women and athletes, this book on African Americans contains biographical profiles of twelve former Members of Congress. The subjects were chosen in 1995 from among former Members of Congress at that time by polling a distinguished advisory board of scholars and current and former Members of Congress.

Professor Shirley Washington, the author of *Outstanding Women Members of Congress*, also wrote this book. She interviewed the living former Members profiled in the following pages, as well as current Member William L. Clay, who generously shared his wealth of knowledge on the subject. Professor Washington and the Society also owe a debt of gratitude to William H. Gray for writing the foreword to this book.

Additional volumes are planned for the series. A collection of twelve essays on Members of Congress who made a contribution to the American environment is in preparation and other topics are being planned. The success of the books in this series has led the Society to institute a youth forum series on the subjects of the publications. A youth forum on Women in Congress was held in Washington, D.C., in 1996 and a forum on Women in Public Service was held in San Francisco in 1997. The first forum on Athletes of Congress was held in Washington, D.C., in 1998. Additional programs will be held in the coming years as the series progresses. Each forum brings student representatives together with current and former leaders to discuss the subjects presented in the *Outstanding Members of Congress Series*.

Clarence J. Brown
President
United States Capitol Historical Society

# *FOREWORD*

The lives of the men and women profiled in this book remind us that a journey of a thousand miles begins with a single step. For the three nineteenth-century pioneers mentioned in the Introduction—Hiram Revels, John Roy Lynch and Robert Smalls—that first step was a giant leap from slavery to freedom. They crossed the chasm that had long separated African Americans from participation in the American political system; but the biographies of Oscar De Priest and Adam Clayton Powell indicate that African-American Members of Congress continued to face major hurdles well into the twentieth century.

I'm flattered to be included in this book with these predecessors and with my colleagues Ed Brooke, Shirley Chisholm, Walter Fauntroy, Gus Hawkins, Parren Mitchell, Andy Young, and especially with those colleagues who are no longer with us, Barbara Jordan, Mickey Leland, and Harold Washington. There are many other notable African-American Congressmen who could have taken our places in this book. In fact, I think that one of the points of the book is that the life stories presented here are representative; just as we represented the people of our constituencies, so do we represent all the African-American Members of Congress listed in the book's appendices.

In writing these biographical essays, the author has succeeded in providing positive role models for today's youth. Each of the men and women profiled in the book demonstrated the value of education as an essential preparation for success in life. Other shared characteristics include a strong commitment to religion, family and the ideals of political, economic and social justice. I hope that many of the young people who read this book will follow in our steps, just as we followed in the steps of those who came before. The journey may not be the same or as difficult, but each person must take that first step.

The Honorable William H. Gray III (D-PA)
House of Representatives, 1979-1991

# INTRODUCTION

## African Americans in Congress, 1870-1901

The twenty-two African-American men elected to the United States Congress from the end of the Civil War to the turn of the twentieth century generally had a number of characteristics in common: almost all were born and raised in slavery in the Southern states that made up the Confederacy; they were committed to ending slavery even if it meant taking up arms; they were brave men with strong family values, dedicated to educating themselves, their children and other slaves; and they were inherently sympathetic to the North and to the Republican Party of Abraham Lincoln. Three of the most representative African Americans of Congress in this period were Hiram Rhodes Revels, John Roy Lynch and Robert Smalls.

### Hiram Rhodes Revels (R-MS; Senate, 1870-71)

*Senator Hiram Rhodes Revels.*

Hiram Rhodes Revels was the first African American elected to the United States Senate. His father was a black Baptist preacher and his mother was a white woman of Scottish descent. Hiram was born on September 27, 1827, in Fayetteville, North Carolina. Although his family was free, his childhood was full of sorrow over the suffering of enslaved blacks. He studied at the Union County Quaker seminary in Indiana and Knox Academy in Galesburg, Illinois, and was ordained a minister in the African Methodist Episcopal Church in Baltimore in 1845.

When the Civil War began, Revels helped organize Maryland's first two black regiments for the Union Army. After the war, he settled in Natchez, Mississippi. Following a term as city alderman in 1868, he was elected to the state Senate in 1869. The state legislature elected him to the United States Senate on January 20, 1870, to fill the unexpired term of former Confederate President Jefferson Davis (Senators were selected by state legislatures until the ratification of the 17th Amendment in 1913). On February 25, 1870, Hiram Revels took his seat as the first African-American United States Senator.

Once in Congress, Revels was appointed to the Committee of Education and Labor and the District of Columbia Committee. He introduced legislation to increase cotton production with an appropriation of more than $2 million to farmers in need and for the repair of levees on the Mississippi River. He advocated integrating the public schools of the District of Columbia and opposed the banning of African-American mechanics from working at the Washington Navy Yard.

When his term in Congress ended in 1871, Revels became president of Alcorn University in Mississippi and later served as Mississippi's interim Secretary of State in 1873. In 1882, he retired and returned to his former church as a pastor in Holly Springs, Mississippi, while teaching theology at Shaw University until his death on January 16, 1901.

## John Roy Lynch (R-MS; House, 1873-77, 1882-83)

(Library of Congress)

*Congressman John Roy Lynch.*

John Roy Lynch was born a slave on September 10, 1847, in Concordia Parish, Louisiana. His father, Patrick Lynch, was a white plantation manager and his mother, Catherine White, a slave. His father died before he was able to purchase the freedom of his wife and three sons. The family was then sold and taken to Natchez, Mississippi.

Lynch had very little formal education; but after his emancipation in 1863, he had the opportunity to attend a night school set up by Northern whites. When the school shut down four months later, he continued to read books and newspapers and to listen to the recitations at a white school across the alley from the photo studio where he worked. During Reconstruction he became active in the local Natchez Republican Club where he spoke in support of ratifying the state's new constitution. In recognition of his devotion to the state, Governor Adelbert Ames appointed him a justice of the peace. In 1869 he won a seat in the Mississippi House of Representatives. In his second term, he became Speaker of the House.

Lynch entered the race for the Sixth Congressional District of Mississippi and won the primary and the general election. Only twenty-six years old, he entered the 43d Congress in 1873 as its youngest member. He was elected to a second term in 1874, but he lost in 1876 to Democrat James R. Chalmers, a former Confederate General. In 1880 Lynch tried to regain his seat, but lost to Chalmers again in a contested election race. This time, however, he successfully appealed the election results to the House, and was seated in the 47th Congress

While in Congress, Lynch introduced bills to donate the Natchez Marine Hospital to the State of Mississippi and to reimburse depositors of the failed Freedman's Savings and Trust Company. He also defended Republican Governor Ames against criticisms of corruption aired by Southern Democrats in Congress. Lynch lost his bid for reelection in 1878 to Democrat Henry S. Van Eaton, a Confederate veteran.

Lynch later was appointed to a position in the Treasury. He went on to become chairman of the Republican State Executive Committee and a member of the Republican National Convention in Chicago in 1884. That same year, Lynch was admitted to the Mississippi Bar. In 1898 he was appointed paymaster of volunteers during the Spanish-American War. In 1901 he was given a presidential appointment as paymaster in the regular army with the rank of captain. He retired from the army in 1911 with the rank of major. In 1912 he moved to Chicago where he wrote a number of books including his biography, which was not published until 1970. He died on November 2, 1939, at his Chicago home and was buried with full military honors in Arlington National Cemetery.

## Robert Smalls (R-SC; House, 1875-79, 1882-83, 1884-87)

Robert Smalls was possibly the most colorful of the Reconstruction Congressmen. Born on April 5, 1839, in Beaufort, South Carolina, to Lydia, his slave mother and Patrick Smalls, his white father and manager of the prosperous McKee Plantation near Beaufort, Robert was a servant in the master's house for most of his younger years. His

*Congressman Robert Smalls.*

mother sought to have her son sent to the McKee's other home because she feared that he might pick up unruly attitudes on the plantation. While serving the McKees in Charleston, South Carolina, he worked as a lamp-lighter and horse driver on the docks. When the Civil War began, he was put to work on the Confederate cotton steamer, *The Planter*. After months of careful planning, when the white officers went ashore, he and the crew stole the steamer, picked up their families and sailed out of the harbor past Fort Sumter toward the Union blockade further down the coast. When the war concluded, he was commissioned a brigadier general in the South Carolina state militia, helping to maintain order during the early years of Reconstruction.

With the Republican Party formally organized in the South, Smalls was elected to the state legislature in 1868. In 1872 he was a delegate to the Republican National Convention in Philadelphia. That same year he won election to Congress from the Third District of South Carolina by a comfortable majority. When he entered the 44th Congress, he was assigned to the Agriculture Committee from which he tried to get federal debt relief for Southerners who had lost their property for nonpayment of wartime taxes. He lost his bid for reelection in 1879 but was reelected in 1882 and served until 1887.

In 1895 Smalls served in the state's Constitutional Convention. Two years later he was appointed customs collector in Beaufort, where he served until he went on the road to campaign for McKinley's reelection. He returned to the post after McKinley's victory and served until 1913. He died on February 22, 1913, at his home in South Carolina.

Hiram Rhodes Revels, John Roy Lynch and Robert Smalls were but three examples of the African Americans who served in the period from the end of the Civil War to the turn of the century. These men were notable for the most obvious and noblest of reasons: making American democracy viable for all of its citizens regardless of skin color. They helped to free not only themselves, but the whole nation from the scourge of injustice. They were true patriots who loved their country and were willing to fight and serve for the sake of freedom and progress. Unfortunately, for twenty-eight years from 1901 to 1929, no African American served in the United States Congress until Oscar De Priest was elected to the House of Representatives from Chicago in 1928.

**For further reading:**

Maurice Christopher, *Black Americans in Congress*, (1976).
William L. Clay, *Just Permanent Interests: Black Americans in Congress, 1870-1992*, (1993).
Julius Eric Thompson, *Hiram R. Revels, 1827-1901: A Biography*, (1980).
Howard N. Rabinowitz, ed., *Southern Black Leaders of the Reconstruction Era*, (1982).
John Roy Lynch, *Reminiscences of an Active Life*, edited by John Hope Franklin, (1970).
Okon Edet Uya, *From Slavery To Public Service: Robert Smalls, 1839-1915*, (1971).
Dorothy Sterling, *Captain of the Planter: The Story of Robert Smalls*, (1958).
Michael L. Cooper, *From Slave to Civil War Hero: The Life and Times of Robert Smalls*, (1994).

*A Currier and Ives print from 1872 pictures the first African-American Members of Congress. Standing (left to right) are Congressmen Robert De Large of South Carolina and Jefferson Long of Georgia. Seated (left to right) are Senator Hiram Revels of Mississippi and Congressmen Benjamin S. Turner of Alabama, Josiah T. Walls of Florida, Joseph H. Rainey of South Carolina and Robert Elliot of South Carolina.*

# Edward William Brooke III

*(October 26, 1919-)*
*Republican-Massachusetts*
*90th-95th Congresses (1967-1979)*

## Moderate Senator From Massachusetts

*Senator Edward W. Brooke.*

Edward W. Brooke III entered the United States Senate in 1967 as the first African American to be seated in that exclusive body since two Mississippi Senators who served during the Reconstruction era following the Civil War. His election reinforced a sense of history, since he too was a Republican as had been Senators Hiram R. Revels (1870-71) and Blanche K. Bruce (1875-81).

The citizens of Massachusetts elected Brooke on the basis of his excellent performance as state attorney general. In so doing, they made him the first popularly elected African-American United States Senator (Revels and Bruce had been elected by the state legislatures). In the Senate, Brooke's reassuring demeanor and moderate politics inspired the public's confidence which grew along with his popularity.

## From Washington to Boston

Brooke was born in Washington, D.C., on October 26, 1919, the only son of Edward Brooke, Sr., a lawyer with the Veterans Administration, and Helen Seldon Brooke, an employee of the Bureau of Engraving and Printing and later the Washington Post Company. Ed and two older sisters were raised in Washington's black middle-class neighborhood of Brookland. The oldest sister died in childhood; but Ed and Helene benefitted greatly from their mother's cultivated outlook. She took them to operas, concerts and outdoor theaters, often in New York City to avoid segregation restrictions in the capital in the 1920s and '30s.

Young Ed Brooke attended elementary and secondary schools in Washington including Dunbar High School. He enrolled in Howard University, majored in chemistry and zoology as a premed course of study and earned a Bachelor of Science degree in 1941. While at Howard he was elected president of Alpha Phi Alpha, a leading African-American fraternity.

World War II began in 1941, the same year that Brooke graduated and was inducted into his university's Reserve Officers Training Corps. He was commissioned as a second lieutenant and assigned to the all-black 366th Combat Infantry Regiment at Fort Devens in Massachusetts. He was assigned the task of defending accused enlisted men and handling special court martial cases. His unit was called into action in Italy where, because of his light skin and fluency in Italian, he was able to work effectively behind enemy lines as a liaison officer with the Italian partisans. He was promoted to captain, won a Bronze Star and the Combat Infantryman's Badge and was honorably discharged.

Edward W. Brooke had lived a fairly privileged happy-go-lucky life. But the sobering experience of war convinced him to do something worthwhile with his life. Two army friends helped him make a career choice between his two major interests—medicine and law. His friends were convinced that he should enter law school after watching him defend prisoners at Fort Devens. They suggested that he study in Boston and set up his practice there. Following their advice, Brooke enrolled at Boston University Law School where he became the editor of the Law Review from 1946 to 1948. He received a master of laws degree in 1950. After graduation, he joined a wartime buddy and opened a combined real estate and law office in Roxbury, a section of Boston. It wasn't long before they began to talk about politics.

When he had taken a vacation in Italy, Brooke had visited the town of Viareggio on the Ligurian Sea, where he had met his future wife, Remigia Ferrari-Scacco, the daughter of a prosperous Genoese merchant. Although he had seen her only five times while in Italy, he had fallen hopelessly in love. He had proposed marriage, but she had rejected him. When he returned home, he kept up the correspondence with Remigia and had proposed to her again by mail. Eventually, she accepted and came to New York. They were married in Boston in June 1947. They had two daughters, Remi and Edwina.

(Courtesy of Edward W. Brooke)

*Senator Brooke with Senate Majority Leader Mike Mansfield.*

## Building a Political Base

Brooke's army buddies persuaded him to run for the state legislature in 1950. Since he had no prior political party affiliation, he filed for both the Democratic and Republican nominations and he was endorsed by the Republican Party. His initial defeat by the Democratic nominee did not deter him from trying again two years later, but again he lost. For the next eight years, Brooke worked to build his reputation as a trusted and capable civic leader. He became state commander and then national judge advocate of AMVETS, a veterans organization.

In 1960 Brooke tried his hand at politics again by running for Massachusetts Secretary of State. In a surprisingly strong showing, he polled a million votes in spite of the Kennedy Democratic presidential blitz in Massachusetts that year. Even though Brooke lost, the margin of defeat had so narrowed (less than 12,000 votes) that he was encouraged to keep trying for political office.

The following year Republican Governor John Volpe appointed Brooke chairman of the Boston Finance Commission, an investigative watchdog agency. Because the city's finances were habitually in disarray, Brooke's name was often in the newspapers as he tried to straighten out the mess. In 1962 he was elected state Attorney General. He was reelected with an even larger vote in 1964—the only Republican to win statewide office in Massachusetts that year. In fact, some Massachusetts Democrats viewed Brooke's victory as the biggest political news in the country at the time.

By 1964 Brooke had established a reputation for seriousness, hard work and friendliness. He made a handsome, dapper appearance in the media and came across as a sincere and honest public servant. He was an excellent Attorney General and the people of Massachusetts appreciated his diligence. He was also lucky and used his political acumen judiciously. His popularity was enhanced when he prosecuted a group of small loan companies involved in price fixing schemes.

Brooke's political tendencies were hard to pin down. He was, for the most part, a moderate Republican who was progressive on social issues and moderate to conservative on fiscal matters. He was quite honest in matters of law and order, and as such, he carried out his duties as attorney general scrupulously; but he was committed to reforming his party to keep it moderate philosophically. Brooke labeled himself a "creative moderate" who rejected extremism as ultimately self-defeating. He explained a good deal of his philosophy in his book, *The Challenge of Change*, which he published in 1966.

At the 1964 Republican National Convention held in San Francisco, Brooke seconded the nomination of William Scranton, Governor of Pennsylvania, for the presidency. Scranton lost the nomination to Senator Barry Goldwater of Arizona, whom Brooke refused to support. However, Goldwater supported Brooke in his race for the United States Senate two years later.

**From Boston to Washington**

When Leverett Saltonstall, the veteran Republican Senator from Massachusetts, retired in 1967, Brooke was nominated to replace him. He made history as the first popularly elected African-American Senator by defeating his opponent, former Democratic Governor Endicott Peabody, in the general election.

Brooke took the oath of office on January 10, 1967. Describing the scene, he revealed, "I felt like a member of the club. They didn't overdo it. They didn't underdo it." But the significance of the historical event did not go unnoticedhis face appeared on the cover of *Time* magazine a month later.

The Republican leadership appointed Brooke to committees with strategic value to his state. He was placed on the Banking and Currency Committee because it acted on much of the legislation involving urban problems. His other assignment, Aeronautical and Space Sciences, was appropriate because of his state's major concentration of aerospace-related industries in the suburbs of Boston.

Though generally cautious, Senator Brooke was not afraid to speak out on issues that struck him as important. He opposed the Vietnam War mainly because it lacked clear objectives in his view. He criticized House Minority Leader Gerald Ford's role in the House decision to deny seating to Adam Clayton Powell, Jr., because he thought it was a Democratic problem best left to that party to resolve. He publicly favored open housing, job training programs and the seating of mainland China in the United Nations. Such views, though out of step with Senate Minority Leader Everett Dirksen (R-IL), reflected Brooke's belief that his party could accommodate differing viewpoints.

Brooke's period in the Senate was pivotal in terms of political change in American history. The civil rights movement had reached a turning point with the rise of the militant rhetoric of Black Power advocates and the public grew increasingly disenchanted with the Vietnam War and Democratic President Lyndon Johnson, whose decent and humane domestic instincts were increasingly distracted by demands on

(Courtesy of Edward W. Brooke)

*Senator Brooke and his Massachusetts colleague, Congresswoman Margaret Heckler, with Vice President Gerald Ford.*

the national treasury by an unpopular war. Internal disorder resulted when a significant segment of society, unhappy with the war, preferred to address a number of festering domestic social problems. The Johnson presidency attempted to address both.

Although critical at times, Senator Brooke did share the President's concerns for the poor and disadvantaged. He sponsored the National Manpower Act of 1968 which matched qualifications of unemployed, underemployed and low-income persons with potential employers. He also concentrated his efforts on low-income and fair housing. He sponsored the 1968 Fair Housing Act after the assassination of Dr. Martin Luther King.

After California Republican Richard Nixon was elected President in 1968, Brooke often criticized the leader of his own party for ignoring the interests of African Americans and the poor. Brooke had been a member of the Johnson administration's Advisory Commission on Civil Disorders, known as the Kerner Commission, which had been established to examine the underlying reasons for the 1968 urban riots. By 1970, the small but growing number of African-American Members of Congress, all Democrats, formed the Congressional Black Caucus. Brooke did not regard himself primarily as an African-American Senator, but as a Senator from a state with a small black population. Since a majority of the voters of his state had voted for him on his merits, he believed it would be wrong to concentrate only on the interests of one segment of the population.

He was sensitive to the problems of his race, however; and his unique position as both an African American and a Republican made him a natural bridge between African-American leaders and the President. He helped arrange a White House meeting on May 25, 1971.

Brooke won reelection in 1972 at the beginning of Nixon's ill-fated second term. With the revelations of the Watergate scandal, Brooke became the first Senator to publicly call for the President's resignation. Brooke also voted against Nixon's nominations to the Supreme Court of Clement Haynsworth, Harold Carswell and William Rehnquist. He supported the Cooper-Church amendments to limit continuing American involvement in Vietnam and he opposed the Cambodian invasion.

When Gerald Ford succeeded Nixon, Brooke often found himself voting in opposition to his own party. He was the floor manager of the 1975 extension of the Voting Rights Act; he led the fight to protect minorities from discrimination in the selection of juries and he voted for a five-year extension of the U.S. Civil Rights Commission. He added the Brooke Amendment to the 1977 International Development Assistance Act that facilitated increased minority business participation. He continued to support or initiate legislation that enhanced educational opportunities, such as the fight he led to save the Student Loan Program for 1977-78. He introduced the Maternal and Child National Health Insurance Act to provide prenatal health care for all children up to 18 and for child immunization against certain diseases. He also opposed the Hyde Amendment which prohibits the use of federal funds for abortion.

During the Carter administration, much of the thrust of Brooke's legislative agenda focused on support of low-income rentals, construction of public housing and the purchase and refurbishment of existing housing units. Brooke did not neglect the military defense of his nation. He accepted the requirements of the reality of the Cold War and America's overseas commitments to such regional alliances as the North

*Senator Brooke (center) with Peter Dominick (left) and Barry Goldwater*
*(right) at televised Senate committee hearing.*

Atlantic Treaty Organization (NATO). He was a member of the Armed Services Committee at one point in his Congressional career as well as the Defense Appropriations Subcommittee.

Brooke defeated a Republican challenger, Avi Nelson, in his 1978 primary, but he lost his seat to Democratic Representative Paul Tsongas in the general election. Another African-American Senator would not be elected until the 1992 election of Carol Moseley-Braun of Illinois.

## Post-Congressional Life

Among the reasons for Senator Brooke's defeat in 1978 were the adverse publicity of his unpleasant but highly public divorce and some questionable, though private, financial matters. By current standards these revelations would not be considered damaging, but Brooke had been for so long a pillar of virtue and such a private man that any hint of scandal was bound to be devastating to his political career. Eventually his reputation and family relations rebounded and he resumed a legal practice in Washington. He remarried and started a new family. Today his business and family interests keep him scurrying between Washington, Martha's Vineyard, and Saint-Martin, an island in the Caribbean where his wife, the former Ann Fleming, has a home.

## Notable Honors and Awards

Brooke had begun accumulating awards as early as 1952 when he was named one of the ten outstanding young men of Greater Boston by the Junior Chamber of Commerce. He has since been the recipient of more than 50 awards and honorary doctoral degrees from, among others, Northeastern University, Worcester Polytechnic Institute, American International College, Emerson College and Portia Law School. He was trustee of Boston University, a chancellor of historical Old North Church, president of the Opera Company of Boston, recipient of a 1967 medal from the National Association for the Advancement of Colored People and a fellow of the American Academy of Arts and Sciences. He also received a Charles Evans Hughes Award for "courageous leadership in governmental service" from the National Conference of Christians and Jews in 1967.

Edward W. Brooke's tenure in the United States Senate from 1967 to 1979 as the first African American elected by the people to that body marked another stage in the development of the promise of American democratic ideals. More importantly, Brooke took his seat because the citizens of Massachusetts had elected him on the basis of his own merit. Moreover, Senator Brooke's service benefitted his constituents, his state and his nation.

## For Further Reading

Edward W. Brooke, *The Challenge of Change: Crisis in Our Two-Party System*, (1966).

William L. Clay, *Just Permanent Interests: Black Americans in Congress, 1870-1992*, (1993).

John Henry Cutler, *Ed Brooke: Biography of a Senator*, (1972).

# *Shirley Anita St. Hill Chisholm*

*(November 30, 1924-)*
*Democrat-New York (12th District)*
*91st-97th Congresses (1969-1983)*

(Library of Congress)

*Congresswoman Shirley Chisholm.*

## Feminist, Teacher and Child Care Advocate

Congresswoman Shirley Chisholm scored a number of firsts during her political career. She was the first African-American woman to win a seat in the New York State Assembly from Brooklyn. She was the first African-American woman to win a seat in the United States House of Representatives; and in 1972, she became the first African American to campaign seriously for the presidential nomination of a major political party.

Chisholm had a reputation as a fearless, ambitious and outspoken maverick. She studied the issues thoroughly and she had utter confidence in her leadership ability. While these qualities were admired in a man, they often cost her dearly for daring to display them as a woman. She was perhaps the quintessential feminist, a serious student of politics who saw no reason why she should hesitate to use her talents in the service of others. Her fearless leadership style was greatly appreciated by supporters and just as ardently disapproved by some of her opponents.

### Growing Up in Barbados and Brooklyn

Shirley Anita St. Hill was born on November 30, 1924, in Brooklyn, New York, the oldest of four daughters of Charles St. Hill and Ruby (Seale) St. Hill. Her father was an emigrant from British Guiana (now Guyana) who worked as an unskilled laborer in a burlap factory in New York. Her mother, an emigrant from Barbados, was employed as a seamstress and a domestic.

Because the family was poor, Shirley's mother took her three-year-old daughter to live with her mother on the family farm in Barbados. Shirley was later joined by two younger sisters who were also sent to live with their grandmother. Shirley and her sisters did not return to Brooklyn until she was eleven. During those formative years, she acquired the soft West Indian accent that would remain with her for life. She benefitted from the British elementary school system and the stern discipline preached by her loving grandmother who instilled in young Shirley the virtues of pride, courage and faith. She also had learned to read and write before she was four years old.

Shirley returned to New York in 1934 to find life very different than it had been in Barbados. Shirley's hard-working parents moved to an apartment in the Bedford Stuyvesant section of Brooklyn where many

17

more blacks lived. She experienced discrimination for the first time when she attended a school in racial transition. Her father was an avid reader who introduced her to the teachings of Marcus Garvey, the West Indian African Nationalist who preached racial pride and black separatism.

Shirley did very well in school. In 1942, she graduated from Girl's High School, a public school in Brooklyn, with an academic diploma and a medal in French. Although she was offered scholarships to Vassar and Oberlin, she turned them down because they were still too expensive for her parents. Instead she chose to attend Brooklyn College, a subway ride away. She graduated cum laude with a degree in sociology in 1946.

A deep concern for the health and social development of young children led her to pursue a career in child care. She went on to earn a masters degree in childhood education from Columbia University in 1952. She also received a teacher certification in nursery, kindergarten and grades one through three, and a professional diploma in supervision and administration in education in 1961.

As a young woman, Shirley St. Hill taught nursery school at Mt. Calvary Child Care Center in New York from 1946 to 1952. She was a school director at the Friend In Need Nursery in Brooklyn from 1952 to 1953 and director of Hamilton-Madison Child Care Center in New York where she was responsible for the administration and supervision of 24 teachers and maintenance of personnel catering to the physical, emotional and intellectual needs of 130 youngsters between the ages of three and ten. She was also an educational consultant for New York's Division of Day Care from 1959 to 1964.

## Entering Democratic Politics in Bedford-Stuyvesant

On October 8, 1949, Shirley St. Hill married Conrad Chisholm, who was nine years older and whom she had met while at Columbia University. He worked for a private security agency that specialized in insurance claims for disability cases, a job that involved a great deal of travel. The Chisholms remained in Bedford-Stuyvesant where Shirley became very active in local politics through the Democratic political clubs.

Because the regular Democratic organization did not welcome the ideas of an African-American woman, Chisholm helped form an independent political club called the Bedford-Stuyvesant Political League (BSPL) and ran a door-to-door canvass and vote-getting campaign. The BSPL effort succeeded in electing the first black judge in Brooklyn history in 1953. In 1954 the BSPL proposed a full slate of black candidates. Although the slate was defeated by the regular organization's candidates, Democratic leaders recognized the potential power of the new organization.

Hoping to win over Chisholm and her followers, the regular party leaders elected her to the party's local board of directors. The old trick of silencing critics by taking them in didn't work; Chisholm continued to criticize the party's policies and to put forth the case for adequate services to the people of her district. Finally, party leaders tired of her behavior and voted Chisholm off the board. She continued to challenge them from the audience and others joined her. Chisholm would not stop until she achieved the goal of black representation at every level of government.

### In the New York State Assembly

By 1964, Chisholm saw a chance to run for a seat in the New York State Assembly. She knew she would be stepping on a few toes of her male colleagues who were not ready to see a woman in a leadership position. One good thing about these gender confrontations was the constant, unequivocal support of her husband.

After a very hard-fought campaign, Chisholm won election to the New York Assembly. Her triumph was not without tragedy; however, because her father died suddenly on the eve of her victory.

Chisholm developed a reputation for being a hard-working, studious and disciplined legislator. Her positions on legislation were based on detailed study from which she seldom wavered. As a member of the Assembly's Education Committee, she continued her fight for underprivileged children and their families.

Of the 50 pieces of legislation she introduced, eight passed, including the 1965 landmark SEEK Program (Search for Elevation, Education and Knowledge) which was designed to help African-American and Puerto Rican high school dropouts who had college potential get into state universities while receiving remedial assistance. The controversial program opened educational opportunities to minorities and compensated for years of inadequate schooling in poor neighborhoods.

Her legislative agenda included helping domestic workers with unemployment insurance, protecting the tenure of female teachers after maternity leave, raising the maximum amounts of money that local school districts could spend on students and providing state aid to day care centers. She voted against public funds for private schools on constitutional grounds.

### "Unbought and Unbossed": Running for the U.S. Congress

Chisholm's constituents appreciated her performance in the state legislature and rewarded her with reelection. By 1967, she focused on running

(AP/Wide World Photos)

*V for Victory: Chisholm and her supporters celebrate news of her election to Congress in 1968.*

for Congress due to the "one-man, one vote" Supreme Court decision requiring the creation of a new Congressional district in central Brooklyn. Chisholm was the first candidate to announce for the June 1968 primary, even though she knew the county Democratic organization would oppose her because she had been too independent and not a team player.

In the tough Democratic primary she ran under the slogan "Unbought and Unbossed" and defeated two opponents, Dolly Robinson, a former labor leader, and the much favored State Senator William C. Thompson. Normally, a primary victory in that district would have been tantamount to winning the general election; but she found herself facing James Farmer, a nationally recognized civil rights leader and former chairman of the Congress of Racial Equality (CORE). Moreover, he was the candidate of both the Republican Party and the Liberal Party, an important third force in New York politics.

Farmer's campaign was well-funded and gained national media attention. Although both candidates stood for similar district concerns regarding employment, housing, education, decentralized local control of schools and opposition to the Vietnam War, in the end Farmer could not overcome Chisholm's advantage of running on the Democratic ticket in an historically Democratic district.

(AP/Wide World Photos)

*Speaker of the House John McCormack administers oath of office to Chisholm, January 3, 1969.*

Moreover, Chisholm proved to be a master campaigner playing on the fact that Farmer was an outsider whereas she had lived in the district and served its people most of her life. She was also helped by Farmer's condescending attitude. His reference to her as "the little schoolteacher" who would not be taken seriously in Congress angered many women voters who happened to outnumber males by a large percentage in the district. In fact, Chisholm specifically appealed to women voters on issues of concern to them. She also reached out to the growing Hispanic population in the area with her ability to speak to them in Spanish. In the election of November 5, 1968, she defeated Farmer by a margin of two-and-a-half to one. In her victory celebration, Chisholm promised supporters that she would not be quiet in Congress.

### "That Disruptive Woman": Chisholm's Congressional Career

On January 3, 1969, Shirley Chisholm made history as the first African-American woman elected to the Congress of the United States when she was sworn into the 91st Congress and took her seat in the House of Representatives. When the Democratic members of the House Ways and Means Committee (the House Democratic majority's Committee on Committees) assigned her to the Agriculture Committee and its subcommittees on rural development and forestry, she protested loudly to the Party Caucus that these panels had no relevance for her Brooklyn constituency. She was widely quoted as having described those who made her assignment as gentlemen whose only knowledge about Brooklyn was that a tree grew in it. It was a bold move for a freshmen Member to question the party leadership, but they relented and reassigned Chisholm to the Veterans Affairs Committee which had more relevance for her constituents.

In March 1970, she gained a seat on the Committee on Organization, Study and Review which recommended reforms that were adopted by the Democratic Caucus in 1971. In the 92d through 94th

Congresses she served on the Committee on Education and Labor. In the 95th through 97th Congresses she was a member of the Rules Committee which controls the flow and amending procedure on all House legislation.

For seven terms (1969-1983), Chisholm championed the social causes that had formed the heart of her career. She co-sponsored a bill calling for a 90-percent federal reimbursement of state welfare programs. As a member of the House consumer affairs study group, she co-sponsored a measure to establish a national commission on consumer protection and product safety. Chisholm proposed funding increases to extend the hours of child care facilities and services to include working mothers of low-income families. She was most proud of her bill passed into law in 1974 that extended minimum wage coverage to domestic workers for the first time. She also urged making Martin Luther King's birthday a national holiday.

Throughout her Congressional career, Chisholm consistently opposed military expenditures and American overseas military involvements. She joined a bipartisan coalition of 15 Members in her first term to introduce legislation to end the draft and create an all-volunteer military. She supported the successful effort in 1971 to repeal Section II of the Internal Security Act of 1950 which required suspected subversives to be interned in emergency detention camps. She chaired the Congressional Black Caucus Task Force on Haitian Refugees. She also opposed apartheid (racial segregation) in South Africa and called for an end to British arms sales to that country.

Representative Shirley Chisholm made history again by seriously campaigning for the Democratic Party's presidential nomination in 1972. Her candidacy caused a split in the Congressional Black Caucus, especially among some of her male colleagues, one of whom referred to her as "that disruptive woman." At every step in her career, Chisholm had faced similar opposition from men who thought her ambitions unattainable because she was a woman. Moreover, her critics claimed Chisholm's candidacy diverted attention from "more important issues." But she was serious about confronting the status quo, and she supported Geraldine Ferraro and Jesse Jackson in their subsequent bids for presidential nominations.

As a legislator, Congresswoman Shirley Chisholm was completely devoted to serving her constituents. She was unafraid to assert herself on behalf of her principles and the well-being of the people of her district, especially the children. She believed that politics should be a tool to effect change and to secure a better way of life for all Americans. Fundamentally, Chisholm was a teacher committed to opening up the political process to people unaccustomed to thinking of themselves as having power. Her electoral battles were always hard-fought and hard-won, but with a celebration of the human spirit.

Following her divorce from Conrad Chisholm in 1977, she married Arthur Hardwick, Jr., a New York state legislator. In 1982 Chisholm announced she would not seek reelection. Her decision was based on a variety of considerations, chief among them was her frustration with the rising tide of conservatism in Congress and the election of President Ronald Reagan. In addition, her second husband had been in a near fatal automobile accident and his health was failing. He died in 1986.

(Library of Congress)

*Congresswoman Chisholm was the first African-American woman to seriously campaign for the presidential nomination of a major political party.*

## Celebrating "The Good Fight"

Since leaving Congress, Chisholm is still fighting "the good fight" as a teacher, lecturer, writer and activist. In 1983, she was appointed Purington Professor at Mt. Holyoke, a women's college in Massachusetts, where she taught politics and women's studies. She co-founded the National Political Congress of Black Women, which sent a delegation of over 100 women to the 1988 Democratic National Convention. She participated in the 1984 and 1988 presidential campaigns of Jesse Jackson because she shared many of his goals for the disadvantaged. President Clinton nominated her to become Ambassador to Jamaica, but she declined for health reasons. She spends much of her retirement writing, lecturing and teaching.

Chisholm has received more than 35 honorary doctoral degrees. She won more than 14 awards from national and international organizations such as the National Press Club and assignments from the United States Department of State and UNESCO. She was honored with the Woman of the Year award from Clairol in 1973 for outstanding achievement in public affairs.

## For Further Reading:

Shirley Chisholm, *Unbought and Unbossed*, (1970).
_____, *The Good Fight*, (1973).
Henry Gilford, *Heroines of America*, (1970).
Catherine Scheader, *Shirley Chisholm: Teacher and Congresswoman*, (1990).

# Oscar Stanton De Priest

*(March 9, 1871-May 12, 1951)*
*Republican-Illinois (First District)*
*71st-73d Congresses (1929-1934)*

*Congressman Oscar De Priest.*

## Symbol of the African American Return to Congress

When Oscar Stanton De Priest took the oath of office as a Member of the 71st Congress on April 15, 1929, he became the first African American elected to that body in the 20th century and the first African American ever to be elected from a Northern city. The last previous black Congressman, George Henry White of North Carolina, left Congress in 1901.

The election of Oscar De Priest also established a pattern of minority representation from Chicago, then America's second largest city, that has produced such African-American legislators as Arthur Mitchell, William Dawson, Ralph Metcalfe, Harold Washington and Cardiss Collins in the House and Carol Moseley-Braun in the Senate.

## Background

Oscar De Priest was born on March 9, 1871, in Florence, Alabama, one of seven children of Alexander De Priest and Mary Karsner De Priest. Seven children made it necessary for his father to supplement his meager earnings as a farmer by using his wagon to haul freight. In addition, his wife took in laundry. In spite of their hard work, the racial climate in Alabama was oppressive and dangerous. As a child, Oscar witnessed several racial attacks; on one occasion he saw a black man dragged from the arms of his weeping wife, shot and hanged in public.

His parents decided to move the family to Salina, Kansas, in 1878. Oscar attended elementary school and took business courses at the Salina Normal School. When he was 17, he and two white boys left school and went to live in Dayton, Ohio. By 1889 he had moved to Chicago, where he was befriended by a white businessman who helped him become an apprentice house painter, plasterer and decorator. The friend later lent Oscar money to open his own successful business painting houses and buildings for the city. On February 23, 1898, he married Jessie Williams. Their son, Oscar Stanton de Priest, Jr., was born on May 24, 1906.

## Pre-Congressional Activities

Life in Chicago offered numerous opportunities for someone as alert and curious as Oscar De Priest. Like most African Americans of his time, he was a Republican because it was the party of the Great Emancipator, President Abraham Lincoln. Once he attended a Republican Party precinct meeting and noticed that he was the only black person there. He quickly grasped the opportunity that politics posed, and before he left the meeting, he had managed to get the job of precinct secretary. In 1904, he ran for Cook County Commissioner and won. He was reelected in 1906.

Politics and business interests formed the focus of De Priest's life. From 1908 until 1915, he spent most of his time speculating in real estate and the stock market. He also developed his own political organization outside the reach of the party regulars, even though William "Big Bill" Thompson, Republican mayor of Chicago, was his mentor. De Priest's organization, consisting mainly of church ministers, small businessmen and personal friends, became his vehicle to build a solid political base.

In 1915, he was elected as Chicago's first African-American alderman with a seat on the city council. He never forgot the poverty of his

(Library of Congress)

*The first African American elected to Congress since 1901, Congressman De Priest took office in 1929.*

childhood which gave him a personal understanding of the plight of his constituents. As an alderman, he was known for providing prompt and efficient municipal services to his constituents. He used his vote and influence to put many blacks on the city payroll as well as to appoint them to white collar jobs in the water and health departments. He also saw to it that he delivered the black vote to the Chicago Republican Party machine by these actions.

In 1917, De Priest resigned from office after being indicted on charges of accepting protection money, a charge not unfamiliar given the nature of the city's politics. Although famed defense attorney Clarence Darrow won his acquittal, De Priest was not able to regain his seat on the city council.

In 1928, Republican Congressman Martin Madden, who had represented the people of the First District for two decades, died suddenly of a heart attack. De Priest had been a longtime ally. He maneuvered the mayor and the committeemen of that district to choose him, as a Madden loyalist, to fill the vacancy until a special election could be held. The district had also undergone a demographic transformation with the steady influx of black migrants from the South now claiming a majority of the population.

In the ethnic machine politics practiced in Chicago, it was viewed as natural for leaders in ethnic neighborhoods to be considered for higher political office, but this had not been the case before for African Americans. De Priest was able to overcome whatever initial opposition there was to his candidacy. Certainly, race was a factor in the election since winning the party nomination was often tantamount to being elected in Chicago. Many white Republicans, however, voted for the white Democratic candidate in the general election. The post-election analysis showed that De Priest carried every black precinct and lost in every white precinct, but because blacks formed the majority, he defeated Democrat Harry Baker and independent William Harrison in the November elections by 3,800 votes in a GOP landslide year.

It had not been an easy victory. Just before the election, a grand jury was convened to investigate some vague corruption charges against De Priest. The Republican machine thought the charges serious enough that De Priest should withdraw from the campaign. He refused because he believed the charges were frivolous. After he won the election, the charges were dropped without explanation.

## Congressional Career

Oscar De Priest took his seat in the 71st Congress on April 15, 1929, but not without controversy as he once again faced opposition because of his race. His problems began even before his arrival in Washington. Rumors were circulated that Southern Congressmen would attempt to prevent him from taking his seat on the basis that he had been indicted.

Ruth Hanna McCormick, another Illinois Republican who had also won a seat in the 71st Congress, worked to remove the last obstacles to seating De Priest. She had a close personal relationship with Alice Roosevelt Longworth, wife of Republican House Speaker Nicholas Longworth and daughter of Theodore Roosevelt. She pleaded for Longworth's influence in the matter.

Speaker Longworth devised a clever strategy to outmaneuver the Southern Democrats. Normally Members had been sworn in by state delegation in alphabetical order. Those members from Alabama, Arkansas, Florida and Georgia would take the oath before those from Illinois. Under the rules, Members already sworn in could challenge the seating of those not yet sworn. To prevent any Southern challenges to De Priest, Longworth called for all Members to stand while he administered the oath as a group. There were other unfriendly acts, however, such as the refusal of George M. Pritchard, newly elected Republican from North Carolina, to occupy a House office next to De Priest.

The most outrageous attempt to snub De Priest centered on a social event at the White House which turned into a tempest in a teapot. The annual Congressional wives tea party hosted by the First Lady at a single gala gathering in the White House was normally a high social event. De Priest presented Republican President Herbert Hoover with a delicate social and racial situation. The Hoovers rejected the option of snubbing Mrs. De Priest as they searched for a compromise. Instead of one setting, the party was divided into four, with Mrs. De Priest invited to the last and the smallest. It was a circumspect arrangement minimizing the possibility of a Southern boycott.

*De Priest campaigned against segregation in the United States Capitol. Here he poses outside the House Restaruant in 1934 after a group of students from Howard University were forcibly ejected.*

Washington, D.C., was in many ways a Southern city. Segregation was the rule in the Nation's Capital—even in the Capitol Building itself. The House of Representatives' private dining room in the Capitol was open to all Members and their guests. Of the two public restaurants, a small one in the basement was designated for black employees and visitors and a larger one on an upper floor was reserved for white employees and visitors. Oscar De Priest was able to use the Members' private dining room regularly, sometimes with guests. However, Morris Lewis, De Priest's private secretary, sometimes ate in the larger public restaurant unchallenged until January 23, 1934, when he and his son were refused service.

Congressman De Priest investigated the incident and discovered that Representative Lindsay C. Warren (D-NC), chairman of the House Accounts Committee had ordered the discriminatory act. De Priest appealed to his colleagues to end the practice and introduced a resolution to investigate whether Warren had exceeded his authority. The Rules Committee, chaired by William B. Bankhead (D-AL), later to be Speaker of the Democrat-controlled House, pigeonholed the resolution, forcing De Priest to seek a petition to bring the entire matter to the floor for debate. He ultimately obtained the 145 signatures required, but not before the issue had become a cause celebre and inspired demonstrations by Howard University students. After floor debate, Chairman Warren's rules were upheld and it would not be until after the Supreme Court's 1952 public accommodations ruling that the House restaurants would be open to all races on a nondiscriminatory basis.

Oscar De Priest was not assigned to the House's more important committees, but rather to the Committee on Enrolled Bills, the Indian Affairs Committee and the Invalid Pensions Committee. But it was significant that he began his Congressional career by confronting some of the same issues that George Henry White fought for at the turn of the century—strong anti-lynching legislation and the implementation of the 14th amendment to reduce Congressional representation for states that disenfranchised its black citizens. Like his predecessor, De Priest more often than not was unsuccessful in persuading the majority of his colleagues to support his measures. Nevertheless, he kept trying and gained some small measure of support.

In ways both large and small, Congressman De Priest kept the issue of racial justice foremost in his legislative agenda. He threatened to block the organization of the House in December 1931 until he was promised governmental action to curb job discrimination in the South. He nominated two black men from his district to the Naval Academy in Annapolis and one to the Military Academy at West Point. De Priest also sought to amend an appropriations bill for the Washington, D.C., public school system to provide additional land for an overcrowded school for blacks. He succeeded in increasing a government grant for a power plant at Howard University from $240,000 to $460,000. He called for an investigation of the House restaurant's treatment of black employees.

In March of 1933 he succeeded in attaching an anti-discrimination rider to a $300-million unemployment relief measure. De Priest also urged the revision of the 14th amendment to assure all citizens equal protection under the law by providing that, if federal courts determined a defendant could not get a fair trial because of race or religion, the accused could ask for a transfer to another jurisdiction. He also introduced a measure to provide $30 monthly pensions to 100,000 ex-slaves over the age of 75.

De Priest did not simply focus on issues pertaining to African Americans. In March 1933, for example, he offered an amendment to a bill that provided the genesis for the Civilian Conservation Corps, an important part of Franklin Roosevelt's New Deal which authorized the President to launch jobs programs to conserve and develop the country's natural resources and alleviate unemployment. He also introduced the bill making Lincoln's Birthday a legal holiday.

## Post-Congressional Activities

The Chicago Congressman was defeated after he voted with his party against Roosevelt's emergency legislation which would have helped the city's depressed Southside. De Priest's famed political acumen had a fatal flaw. He failed to note the profound change taking place as African Americans, because of their desperate economic plight during the Great Depression, left the Republican Party of Lincoln and McKinley to switch to the Democratic Party of Franklin Delano Roosevelt. Arthur Mitchell, a Roosevelt supporter, defeated De Priest in 1934 election.

De Priest returned to Chicago and real estate in partnership with his son. He made a brief reentry into politics as a delegate to the Republican National Convention in 1936 and as a member of the Chicago City Council from 1943 to 1947. His failing health led to his retirement from business and politics. He died on May 12, 1951, at the age of 80.

De Priest deserves to be remembered as a hero of Congress because he assumed a duty of representation that went beyond representing those who had voted for him, but also included the millions of African Americans who could not vote for anyone like him. Nevertheless, he did not shrink from taking on such a tremendous burden because he knew that he was the only national African-American leader whose credentials could not be seriously questioned.

De Priest also assumed heroic proportions by his very presence in an institution that until then had not faced up to the contradiction between the evolving ideals of a democratic republic and the reality of inequality and segregation that existed both inside Congress and in the larger society it represented. Like a weather vane, he was a symbol of things to come.

## For Further Reading

William L. Clay, *Just Permanent Interests: Black Americans in Congress, 1870-1992*, (1993).

David S. Day, "Herbert Hoover and Racial Politics: The De Priest Incident," *Journal of Negro History* 65 (Winter 1980): 6-17.

Nicholas P. Georgiady, et al., *Oscar De Priest: American Negro Statesman*, (no date).

Kenneth Eugene Mann, "Oscar Stanton De Priest: Persuasive Agent for the Black Masses," *Negro History Bulletin* 35 (October 1972): 134-37.

Elliott M. Rudwick, "Oscar De Priest and the Jim Crow Restaurant in the U.S. House of Representatives," *Journal of Negro Education* 35 (Winter 1966): 77-82.

# Walter Edward Fauntroy

*(February 6, 1933-)*
*Democrat-District of Columbia*
*92d-101st Congresses (1971-1991)*

## Home Rule Advocate

(Library of Congress)

*Delegate Walter Fauntroy.*

Walter E. Fauntroy was first elected in 1971 as the District of Columbia's non-voting delegate to the House of Representatives. In the two decades he served in that capacity in Congress, he helped to secure a limited form of home rule for the people of the Nation's Capital. If it had been adopted, an amendment to the Constitution he introduced in 1978 would have granted the District the same representation as a state. Home rule was his singular, though unsuccessful, preoccupation during most of his tenure and his most enduring contribution to the District of Columbia.

### An Education in Religion and Civil Rights

Walter Edward Fauntroy was born on February 6, 1933, in Washington, D.C. He was the fourth of seven children born to William T. Fauntroy and Ethel Vine Fauntroy. His father was a clerk in the U.S. Patent Office and his mother was a part-time seamstress.

Because he was a small child, he had to try harder and use sports to gain the respect of his peers. The local Police Boys Club provided him facilities to play a variety of sports such as boxing, baseball, basketball and football. Shaw, the poor working-class neighborhood where he grew up, had the usual vices present in many inner city neighborhoods. He was drawn to the New Bethel Baptist Church, a neighborhood sanctuary, as a haven from such perils.

Fauntroy did well as a student at Dunbar High School. He graduated in 1952, having already decided that he wanted to enter the ministry. His church paid his first year's tuition at Virginia Union University. Again he did well, graduating cum laude with a bachelor of arts degree in 1955. He then attended Yale University Divinity School on a full scholarship and received a bachelor of divinity degree in 1958. Upon graduation, he was offered a deanship of the Divinity School, but he declined to accept the pastorship of the New Bethel Baptist Church in the District of Columbia, where he has remained ever since. On August 3, 1957, he married Dorothy Simms whom he met when they were both students. They had two children, Marvin and Melissa.

From his youth, Fauntroy viewed religion as something more vibrant than the traditional preaching and singing on Sunday morning. For him, religion was a more active part of daily life. In that regard, it was not surprising that Dr. Martin Luther King, whom he had met in 1954, became his political and spiritual mentor as well as his friend.

Fauntroy was a product of his times. Like many young black Baptist ministers, he was drawn to King's movement. Fauntroy took part in the demonstrations, marches, sit-ins and negotiations of the civil rights movement in the 1960s. His ministry and activities made him a reliable ally. He was named director of the Washington Bureau of the Southern Christian Leadership Conference (SCLC) and acted as its chief lobbyist for passage of the Civil Rights Act of 1964 and the Voting Rights Act of 1965. In addition, he helped organize the freedom rides and protest marches of the early '60s. The highlight of his organizing skills was preparing the famous March on Washington in August 1963 which attracted 200,000 people from all walks of life to hear Martin Luther King's "I Have a Dream" speech.

## From Community Leader to Delegate to Congress

After the 1964 civil rights legislation passed Congress, President Lyndon Johnson appointed Fauntroy as vice-chairman of the White House Conference to Fulfill These Rights in 1966. The appointment recognized Fauntroy's role in the passage of the legislation. After Dr. Martin Luther King's assassination on April 4, 1968, Fauntroy worked closely with other SCLC leaders to carry out King's plan to launch a Poor People's Campaign to petition Congress to enact national anti-poverty legislation.

Walter Fauntroy cared deeply about the plight of the poor. He deplored what often happened to poor people under federally legislated urban renewal programs. Fauntroy and a group of ministers founded a private agency which sought to include local residents in the renewal process. The agency started a neighborhood housing scheme financed by the churches with Fauntroy as its first unpaid director. He then accepted his first political office when President Johnson appointed him vice-chairman of the District of Columbia Council from 1967 to 1969.

On September 9, 1970, President Nixon signed a bill giving the District of Columbia a nonvoting delegate in the House of Representatives. The delegate could represent the citizens of the District, serve on Congressional committees and introduce legislation, but could not vote on the House floor. Two weeks after the bill was signed, Fauntroy announced his candidacy for the Democratic nomination for the post. His chief support came from the District's black pastors and civil rights leaders. On January 12, 1971, he won the primary election with 44 percent of the vote out of a crowded field. Reverend Fauntroy took his campaign directly to the people on walking tours of the city. His platform called for federally-funded day care centers, improved higher education facilities, mass transit subsidies and a guaranteed annual income at levels of decent support for the working poor and the seasonally unemployed. He captured 59 percent of the vote to Republican John Nevius' 25 percent.

(AP/Wide World Pho

*Fauntroy, Washington director of the Southern Christian Leadership Conference, speaks to reporters after meeting with President Lyndon B. Johnson in the White House.*

## Campaigning for Home Rule for the District of Columbia

Fauntroy had campaigned for election on a home rule platform. The city was governed by a mayor and city council appointed by the President, not elected by the citizens. Delegate Fauntroy hoped to change that.

Sworn into the House of Representatives on April 19, 1971, Fauntroy immediately set out to push a home rule bill through the House

(AP/Wide World Photos)

*House Majority Leader Jim Wright (D-TX) gives Delegate Fauntroy a victory ride after Washington won the NFC championship game over Dallas in 1983.*

District of Columbia Committee, but he knew he would have to build support for it. He was joined by Republican Senator Edward W. Brooke, himself a native Washingtonian, and the only African American in the Senate, to create nonpartisan citizens committees to lobby Congress.

John McMillan (D-SC), chairman of the House Committee on the District of Columbia, opposed home rule. Fauntroy, through the black churches in the chairman's state, organized black voters against McMillan. The chairman was subsequently defeated for reelection for many reasons, not the least of which was his failure to carry the black vote.

In January 1973, the House Democratic Committee on Committees awarded Fauntroy seniority on legislative committees despite his nonvoting status. He subsequently became chairman of the Committee on the District of Columbia's Subcommittee on Judiciary and Education. He also became a member of the Committee on Banking, Finance and Urban Affairs and was chairman of its Subcommittee on International Development Institutions and Finance.

Fauntroy's legislative activities covered both domestic and international matters. He submitted a proposal to establish a national sickle cell anemia program, to impose sanctions on heroin-producing countries and to make land on the Bolling-Anacostia military reservation available for the construction of civilian housing projects and hospitals. He co-sponsored anti-drug bills as a member of the House Select Committee on Narcotics. In international affairs, he supported efforts to end minority rule in South Africa and to assist economic development in Haiti. During the 97th Congress (1981-83), he was elected Chairman of the Congressional Black Caucus (CBC).

During the 1972 presidential campaign, Fauntroy ran as the District's favorite son candidate. This allowed him to control a bloc of voting delegates to use at the Democratic National Convention to support whichever presidential candidate came closest to supporting the CBC program and home rule for the District of Columbia. When Senator George McGovern (D-SD) pledged his support, Representatives Fauntroy, William Clay (D-MO) and Louis Stokes (D-OH) cast the votes they controlled to help McGovern win the nomination on the first ballot.

All the maneuvering within the Democratic Party came to naught when McGovern lost the election by a wide margin to Republican candidate Richard Nixon. Nevertheless, late in 1973 a compromise home rule bill passed and was signed by President Nixon. The D.C. Self-Government and Governmental Reorganization Act allowed Washington residents to elect their city council and mayor; however, Congress retained a veto over the District's finances.

Delegate Fauntroy accepted the home rule act as the best he could achieve given the political mood of the Democratic Congress. Having helped the federal city get a degree of local self-government, he continued to work for D.C. statehood for the rest of his career in Congress. He continually reminded his colleagues that the then 760,000 residents of the Capital outnumbered the seven least populous states, all of which each had two votes in the Senate and one or two in the House. Fauntroy submitted a proposed amendment to the Constitution which would give the District the status of a state in the election of Congressional representatives, the allocation of presidential electors and the ratification of Constitutional amendments. The House passed the proposed amendment in March 1978 by a vote of 287 to 127. The Senate con-

(AP/Wide World Photos)

*Senator Pete Domenici (R-NM) and Fauntroy compete in bicycling in 1975, previewing competition for the title of "King of Capitol Hill."*

curred; but the amendment was never ratified by the required three-fourths of the states.

Reverend Fauntroy had other equally pressing concerns overseas. He worked to bring an end to the South African system of racial oppression known as apartheid. Violence in South Africa triggered a dramatic protest by a small, but influential group of African Americans, including Fauntroy, who began a sit-in at the South African Embassy on the eve of Thanksgiving, 1985. The protests and arrests became a daily occurrence and helped set the stage for the Comprehensive Anti-apartheid Acts of 1985 and 1986 which were subsequently passed by Congress over the veto of President Ronald Reagan. As a result of American and world pressure, the South African government freed its political prisoners and held the free and fair elections which brought Nelson Mandela to that nation's presidency.

## Post-Congressional Career

Fauntroy decided to give up his seat in Congress in an unsuccessful bid for the 1990 Democratic nomination for mayor of the District of Columbia. Since leaving Congress at the end of his term in 1991, the former delegate has opened a consulting firm devoted to economic development at home and abroad. He continues in a variety of activities on the board of directors of the Martin Luther King, Jr., Center for Social Change in Atlanta and the Southern Christian Leadership Conference. He is a member of the Yale University Council, a member of the board of trustees of Virginia Union University and remains pastor of New Bethel Baptist Church. In 1993 he served as the chairman of the 30th anniversary of the famous 1963 March on Washington.

Reverend Fauntroy was honored with the Hubert H. Humphrey Humanitarian Award from the National Urban Coalition in 1983. He has been honored by a number of honorary degrees from such institutions of higher learning as Georgetown University Law School, Yale University and Virginia Union University, among others.

When the voters of the District of Columbia elected Walter E. Fauntroy as their delegate to the House of Representatives in 1971, he truly became their Congressman in action and sentiment. As a result of his efforts, the District of Columbia attained a degree of home rule. He was truly an outstanding Congressional Delegate, serving his constituents and the nation for two decades during which he gave voice to the democratic impulses of freedom-loving people throughout the world.

## For Further Reading

William Clay, *Just Permanent Interests: Black Americans in Congress, 1870-1992*, (1993).
Walter E. Fauntroy, "The Triple Whammy: Help Change This System," *Vital Speeches of the Day*, September 15, 1988, pp. 706-10.

# William Herbert Gray III

*(August 20, 1941-)*
*Democrat-Pennsylvania (Second District)*
*96th-101st Congresses, 1979-1991*

*Congressman William H. Gray III.*

## The Coalition Builder

**W**illiam H. Gray III attained two highly significant positions during the 12 years he served in the world's foremost legislative body—the United States House of Representatives. He held the important leadership positions of chairman of the influential House Budget Committee and Democratic whip, the third highest majority party post in the House. Gray became the highest ranking African American in Congress because, as a *New York Times* reporter noted, he was "adept at building coalitions and unafraid to risk rejection."

### Childhood and Education

William Herbert Gray III was born in Baton Rouge, Louisiana, on March 12, 1941. He and his sister, Marion, were the children of Dr. William H. Gray, Jr., and Hazel Yates Gray. Dr. Gray had earned his doctorate from the University of Pennsylvania and subsequently became a minister and college president in Florida. The family moved to North Philadelphia, Pennsylvania, in 1949 when Dr. Gray became pastor of the Bright Hope Baptist Church founded by his father in 1925. Mrs. Hazel Gray was a high school teacher and a college dean at different times in her life.

Young Bill Gray attended elementary and secondary schools in Philadelphia. He graduated from Simon Gratz High School in 1959 and earned a bachelor's degree in sociology at Franklin and Marshall College in Lancaster in 1963. During his senior year in college, Gray served as an intern to Pennsylvania Congressman Robert N. C. Nix.

Gray's father noted that his son showed little interest in the ministry until late in college. Gray continued his education by enrolling in Drew Theological Seminary in New Jersey where he earned a master of divinity degree in 1966. He continued his graduate studies in theology at several universities, including the University of Pennsylvania, Temple and Oxford. He earned another master's degree in theology from Princeton Theological Seminary in 1970.

After completing his theological studies, Gray became a pastor at Union Baptist Church in Montclair, New Jersey, and later was installed as its senior minister by Dr. Martin Luther King, who had been a frequent family guest when Bill Gray was a boy. When his father died, Gray replaced him as pastor of the Bright Hope Baptist Church in Philadelphia.

From 1970 to 1974, Gray retained his academic interests by teaching at several area colleges, including Rutgers University, Montclair State

College, Jersey City State College and St. Peter's College in New Jersey. In 1971, he married Andrea Dash, a marketing consultant. They had three boys: William H. IV, Justin Yates, and Andrew Dash.

Gray's life continued to center around religion and academics; but as time went on he became more and more interested in politics as a tool for change. He realized that he had considerable backing from the large black churches in Philadelphia. (His own congregation numbered 4,000 members). Gray also had become active in civil rights. He assisted in the founding of a nonprofit organization, Union Housing Corporation, which built affordable housing projects for low income families in the community. He also developed a mortgage plan in Philadelphia which enabled residents in poor neighborhoods to obtain mortgages for their homes.

## Congress: Off to a Fast Start

In 1976 Gray decided to challenge his former employer, Congressman Robert Nix, and lost a close race in the Democratic primary. However, he successfully challenged Nix in the 1978 primary and won in the general election by a wide margin. He was sworn in as the Representative of Pennsylvania's Second District to the 96th Congress on January 3, 1979.

Maryland Congressman Parren Mitchell, who was leaving the House Budget Committee, was anxious that he be replaced by another member of the Congressional Black Caucus. Mitchell successfully maneuvered Gray's appointment to the committee. Gray was a quick study for a freshman Congressman. He made good contacts that gave him a head start on learning the ways of the institution. He befriended power brokers such as John P. Murtha, Democrat from Pennsylvania, and won a coveted seat on the Democratic Steering and Policy Committee, a key party panel which determines Democratic House committee assignments.

(Courtesy of William H. Gray)

*Known as the most powerful African-American in Congress, Gray was often asked to be a spokesman for the Democratic Party. In this press conference he is accompanied by (from left to right): Richard Gephardt, Jack Brooks, Donald Payne, Tom Foley and David Bonior.*

Gray was appointed to two other committees as well—Foreign Affairs and the District of Columbia. As a member of Foreign Affairs,

*In 1989 Gray became the first African American to be elected House majority whip. Here he poses with fellow Democratic Congressman Kweisi Mfume (MD), Steny Hoyer (MD) and David Bonior (MI).*

Gray succeeded in establishing a new development program, the African Development Foundation, whose purpose is to provide direct delivery of American aid to villages on the African continent. It was a remarkable feat. He was, indeed, off to a fast start.

In his second term, Gray made a number of important moves. He gained a coveted seat on the Appropriations Committee and served as vice chair of the Congressional Black Caucus. Gray relinquished his seat on the Appropriations Committee in order to reclaim a seat on the Budget Committee in 1983. In the same year, he sponsored legislation that would guarantee minority and female participation in businesses and black colleges in programs administered by the Agency for International Development. He was one of the earliest members to warn of the impending food crisis in Ethiopia. He sponsored a bill which Congress passed in 1984 to provide emergency food aid to that African nation.

**Congressional Party Leadership: House Budget Chair**

Representative Gray's career in the House continued to rise due to his knowledge and appreciation for the workings of the institution, his own self-confidence and his ability to reach out beyond his natural base to build coalitions in order to pass effective legislation. He had a clear idea of what he wanted to achieve and went after it with skill. He began his campaign for the chairmanship of the House Budget Committee in 1984.

Under House rules, members of the Budget Committee were allowed a maximum period of service of eight years: six as a member and another two as chairman. The sitting chairman, Jim Jones of Oklahoma, whose term would end at the close of 1984, sought to change the rules in order to serve another term. When the rules change was defeated, it opened the chairmanship to any eligible member; and Gray had garnered the necessary votes.

When Congressman Gray became chairman of the Budget Committee in January 1985, as the first African-American Member to hold the post, he was often referred to as "the most powerful black Member of Congress." Certainly, his accomplishments were a source of pride for his constituents, 2,000 of whom poured into the Capitol for the short ceremony installing him as chairman of the committee. The gathering had been organized by his church and was an impressive show of support.

At the time Gray was elected chairman, some Democrats feared that putting a black Northeastern liberal in such a key post was the wrong signal for their party. They believed the party needed to appeal more to more fiscally conservative white voters in the South and West to counter Republican President Ronald Reagan's support in those areas. By early 1985, overcoming concern that a black liberal could not be a serious budget-cutter, Gray had put together a diverse regional and ideological coalition. The chairman's support mirrored the unity he would help bring to the once-fractured party over the next four years

Gray defied expectations by earning the trust of moderate Democrats. Two of his most enthusiastic supporters were "boll weevils" (Southern Democratic supporters of President Reagan's policies), Texans Marvin Leath and Charles W. Stenholm (the latter described Gray as a man with "West Texas tractor-seat common sense").

Chairman Gray also engendered trust among Republican members. Although differing in economic philosophy, Gray joined forces with Republican Representative Jack Kemp of New York on several issues such as tax-free "enterprise zones" for blighted urban areas. Another Republican committee member, Vin Weber of Minnesota, explained why he broke ranks with his party to vote for Gray's budget. He remembered that Gray had chaired a hearing in his district on farm problems. These praises did not disguise Republican complaints about the House budget system that virtually excluded them from any input in writing the budget; but generally they did not blame Gray for the way the system worked.

Chairing one of the most partisan committees in Congress, Gray had to operate within fairly narrow guidelines. Therefore, leadership style played a critical role. Gray was extremely task oriented, and tried to prevent confrontation. With almost infinite patience, he exhibited remarkable skills at avoiding and managing conflict.

Gray's tenure as Budget Chairman was not without its own inner tension. In trying to hammer out a budget resolution for fiscal year 1987, he had to face additional difficulties complicated by the Gramm-Rudman-Hollings Amendment, a budget-balancing law that mandated automatic budget cuts across the board unless certain deficit-reduction targets were met. Gray bitterly opposed the law which he regarded as "horrendous public policy, violating the most fundamental principles of Congressional responsibility and accountability." Gray regarded his own efforts as deficit cutting with compassion.

The four budgets written under Gray's auspices received a total of 919 Democratic votes in support and only 77 in opposition. It was an impressive display of party unity compared with the House Democrats' disarray in the early years of the Reagan administration. Gray had won the gratitude of his party leaders. The fiscal 1987 budget resolution was adopted by the full House by a 245-179 vote. Democrats voted 228-19 for the plan. Only in Gray's first year as chairman had there been a larger margin (234-15).

(Courtesy of William H. Gray)

*Gray's resignation from Congress in 1991 came as a surprise. The mantle of leadership passed to Kweisi Mfume (right), chairman of the Congressional Black Caucus.*

## House Democratic Leadership: Majority Whip

Beginning in mid-1987, Gray campaigned to succeed Richard Gephardt (D-MO) as chairman of the House Democratic Caucus, a contest that was still more than a year away. He sought to persuade his colleagues of his ability to bring together the often fractious interests that existed nationally among Democrats. He was given ample opportunity to display his coalition-building skills—or fail to—as chairman of the party's platform drafting committee at the 1988 Democratic Presidential Nominating Convention.

As a result, Gray was overwhelmingly elected chairman of the House Democratic Caucus on December 5, 1988, and took office in early January 1989. The new post was yet another rung up the ladder into the highest levels of the Democratic House leadership. Gray performed well in that post for just six months, when an unexpected opening for House majority whip developed in June 1989 with Congressman Tony Coehlo's resignation.

The majority whip performs the critical function of gathering information on how Members will vote on pending legislation. It is also the whip's duty, using a variety of methods, to persuade Members of his party to vote with the party's position.

The election of Bill Gray to the post of House majority whip was helped by the constant, unwavering support of his constituents. It also demonstrated the gratitude of the party's leaders for the fine job he performed in the assignments he had been given. His coalition-building skills had proven to be impressive and his successes had helped to broaden the base of his party. Gray liked to think of himself as a facilitator bringing consensus among Members from varied backgrounds and political perspectives. His ascendance to the most prominent leadership post in the House ever held by an African American was a genuine success story for him personally, his constituents, his party and the institution.

## A Puzzling Decision

Congressman Gray performed his role as majority whip well. In time, Capitol Hill insiders speculated that he could become the first African-American Speaker of the House. However; on June 20, 1991, Gray stunned both rivals and supporters by announcing his resignation from Congress. He explained that he would be heading the United Negro College Fund. Gray stated, "I'm giving up political power to have a very big impact on the education of black young people throughout this decade."

Gray's departure notice fueled vague rumors of scandal prompted by unspecified investigations of his office staff by the Justice Department. The Attorney General finally ended the speculation by clearly stating that Gray was not the target of the investigation. The lack of substance to the rumors made Gray's resignation all the more puzzling to cynical observers who could not understand why anyone would voluntarily give up such a promising Congressional career. But Gray's decision was not all that surprising given his educational and theological background. The new position was a rare opportunity to take a journey home: "I come from a family where my father was president of two historically black colleges. My mother was a dean of students at a black college, and my sister teaches now at a black college. So that's really my roots."

## Post-Congressional Career

Former Congressman Gray has thrown himself into his new position with enthusiasm and joy; yet he has remained vitally interested in national and international affairs. In 1994, President Bill Clinton called upon him to serve as the presidential advisor on Haiti in an effort to restore democracy to that troubled island nation.

Gray has received more than 50 awards and honors from various colleges and civic organizations. The Black President's Roundtable Association awarded him its Distinguished Leadership Award for his political acumen, commitment to minority business enterprise and pursuit of justice.

In the 12 years he served in the House of Representatives, William H. Gray III achieved a level of leadership unprecedented among African-American Members of Congress. In reviewing the long and troubled history of African Americans in Congress in his book *Just Permanent Interests* (1993), Congressman William Clay (D-MO) has noted the turning point marked by Gray's leadership posts. Gray's lasting accomplishment was the creation of "the perception among many white Democrats that blacks were entitled to representation in that elite leadership group. Why they decided to re-evaluate their life-long opposition to blacks' giving direction and leadership—and why they reversed their once strongly held conviction . . . —is far beyond my powers of comprehension. . . . But I am happy we have come this far."

**For Further Reading**

William L. Clay, *Just Permanent Interests: Black Americans in Congress, 1870-1992,* (1993).
William H. Gray, "Should the U.S. Provide Aid to Anti-Government Forces in Angola?" *Congressional Digest* (April 1986): 119-23.

# Augustus Freeman Hawkins

*(August 31, 1907-)*
*Democrat-California (21st and 29th Districts)*
*88th-101st Congresses (1963-1991)*

## Proponent of Economic Fairness

*Congressman Augustus F. Hawkins.*

If longevity in office and legislative accomplishments equal experience, then Augustus F. Hawkins was probably the most experienced African-American Congressman in his nation's history. He compiled an enviable record during 56 years of public service in the California State Assembly and the U.S. Congress. He sponsored more than 100 laws during 28 years in California and more than 17 federal laws during 28 years in Congress. Most of these legislative accomplishments were devoted to achieving economic opportunities for all segments of American society.

### Family Values and Public Service

Hawkins was born on August 31, 1907, in Shreveport, Louisiana. He was the youngest of five children born to Nyanza Hawkins, a British-born immigrant pharmacist and former African explorer, and his wife, Hattie Freeman Hawkins. The Hawkins family's relocation to Los Angeles in 1918 was partly motivated by his father's concern that his mischievous son would get into trouble in the oppressive racial environment of the early twentieth-century American South.

The family valued hard work and education. Gus (a nickname that has stuck with him all his life) began working even while attending Jefferson High School in Los Angeles. After graduation in 1926, he continued to work during his years at the University of California at Los Angeles. He graduated in 1931 with a bachelor's degree in economics. Although he really wanted to continue his studies in civil engineering, the Great Depression of the 1930s forced him to go into the real estate business with his brother.

Politics became the focus of Hawkins's life when he took courses in the Institute of Government at the University of Southern California and worked as a Young Democrat for Franklin D. Roosevelt's 1932 presidential campaign. Aroused in 1934 by gubernatorial candidate Upton Sinclair's famous slogan, "End Poverty in California" (EPIC) and his own growing interest in politics, Hawkins challenged a 16-year Republican incumbent for a seat in the state legislature. He won a decisive victory under the slogan of a "new broom" needed for his predominantly African-American and Hispanic district in Los Angeles.

Hawkins served in the state legislature with distinction from 1935 to 1963. He quickly established a political reputation as a diligent, hard-working legislator. Quiet, conscientious and efficient, he rose to become one of the most powerful members of the assembly. He chaired the Rules Committee and the Joint Legislative Organization Committee, the highest ranking committee in the state legislature. In the process, Hawkins built an impressive record supporting legislation concerning slum clearance, low-cost housing, domestic workers compensation, disability insurance for farm laborers, apprenticeship training and child care.

The most outstanding achievement of Hawkins's career in the California Assembly was passage of the Fair Employment Practices Act of 1959 for which he had worked since 1945. The act was a tribute to his steadfast dedication to providing economic justice for working people by opening opportunities for everyone willing to work to have a good-paying job. Hawkins's compassion for the poor and for working people was a product of his own experience during the Great Depression and the values instilled by his family. Much of his career in Congress was based on a belief in the economic empowerment of the people and the development of their families and communities.

Hawkins's first wife, Pegga Adeline Smith, who died in 1966, was an aspiring concert singer when they married on August 28, 1945, but she gave up her career to manage a local fabric store in order to help with her husband's political campaigns. In 1977, he married Elsie Taylor. Hawkins never served in the Armed Forces because, like many men his age, he was too young for World War I and too old for World War II. An active man now in his late eighties, he attributes his longevity and vigor to a personal dislike for tobacco and television.

## Pursuing His Goals at the National Level

In 1959 Hawkins narrowly lost a bid to become Speaker of the California Assembly. This defeat helped convince him to run for Congress. After over two decades in the state legislature, it was time to pursue his goals at the national level.

At age 55, Hawkins campaigned in 1962 with the support of President John F. Kennedy for a seat in Congress from the mostly African-American and Hispanic 21st District in Los Angeles. Winning by a landslide, he became the first African American elected to Congress from west of the Rocky Mountains. He joined fellow Democratic Representatives William L. Dawson (IL), Adam Clayton Powell, Jr. (NY), Charles Diggs (MI) and Robert Nix (PA) as the only African Americans in Congress at the time.

(AP/Wide World Photos)

*Hawkins shortly after he took office in 1963 as the first African American elected from west of the Rocky Mountains.*

Hawkins's stated purpose in running for Congress was that he wanted to continue pursuing issues of paramount importance at the national level. "I ran for Congress because many of the issues with which I am deeply concerned, . . . transcend to the national level," Hawkins has said. "I felt that as a Congressman I could do a more effective job than in the [state] Assembly."

## A Low Key Approach to Congressional Leadership

When Gus Hawkins entered the 88th Congress in January 1963, he was assigned to the House Education and Labor Committee. Powell, the charismatic Harlem Congressman and preacher, was the committee's chairman. Even though Hawkins became chairman of the same committee years later, he rejected Powell's more flamboyant style. Gus preferred to work quietly. It was not part of his nature to engage in flashy oratory. Although he attributed his low-key style to his background in engineering, he was a tenacious fighter for his political values.

Hawkins chaired several committees during his 28 years in Congress. In the 97th Congress (1981-83) he was chairman of the Joint House-Senate Committee on the Library as an extension of his Chairmanship of the Committee on House Administration, the panel responsible for managing the affairs of the House of Representatives in areas relating to personnel operations and election laws. The following Congress he chaired the Joint Committee on Printing but became the chair of more important Committee on Education and Labor.

As the Education and Labor Committee's second African-American chairman, Hawkins headed the House's second largest committee (next to Energy and Commerce) with numerous subcommittees, a 35-member professional staff and a 100-person support staff. It is the chairman's job to oversee federal education and labor programs and to enact legislation for projects whose budgets have exceeded 60 billion dollars a year.

Hawkins became chairman of Education and Labor in his twenty-second year in Congress at age 77. When Powell had been chairman, the Democratic majority in Congress and Democratic Presidents Kennedy and Johnson had supported appropriations for education and jobs programs. A strong economy had also made possible such federal spending programs. But times had changed when Hawkins became chairman. Years of inflation and federal spending for "guns and butter"—defense and domestic programs—meant that less federal funds were available and resulted in greater opposition to spending and more support for budget-cutting. Hawkins also had to contend with the phenomenon of divided government—Democratic majorities in Congress but Republican incumbents in the presidency (Ronald Reagan and George Bush). As a result, a kind of silent political war was waged between the chairman of a powerful House committee and the executive branch of the federal government.

### Employment and Education Programs: Humphrey-Hawkins and Beyond

The Humphrey-Hawkins Full Employment Act of 1978 was Hawkins's best known and most ambitious legislative accomplishment. Conceived in 1974-75 with Senator (and former Vice-President) Hubert Humphrey (D-MN), the bill committed the federal government to a policy of a decent job to everyone who wanted one by requiring the President and all federal agencies to direct their fiscal policies toward achieving full employment.

The Humphrey-Hawkins bill originally targeted a reduction in unemployment levels to three percent within 18 months. Critics attacked the bill as inflationary and a dangerous enhancement of federal government power. Because Sen. Humphrey died before final passage of the bill, it fell to Hawkins to lead it through Congress.

Between its introduction in 1976 and final passage in the fall of 1978, the Humphrey-Hawkins bill was substantially weakened. The final bill permitted the President to alter unemployment goals and did not provide a mechanism for reducing unemployment. The law has been seen as largely symbolic both of the government's commitment to full employment and its inability to achieve it. As such, the law has been a disappointment to Hawkins, even though Lincoln University awarded him an honorary Doctor of Laws degree in 1978 for his work on education and labor-related matters including the Humphrey-Hawkins Act.

Hawkins himself does not regard the Full Employment Act as the highlight of his legislative career. He is proudest of his efforts in the areas of education and job training. His greatest sense of accomplishment came from bills dealing with education, such as the School Improvement Act of 1988, also known as the Hawkins-Stafford Act. This act amended the original Elementary and Secondary School Act of 1965 to incorporate the principle that students had to show academic improvement in order for their schools to continue to receive federal aid. In Hawkins's opinion, if the act had been properly implemented, it would have done more to improve the level of American education than any other measure.

The School Improvement Act was but the most recent of Hawkins's measures to improve educational opportunities. In 1974 he wrote the Juvenile Justice and Delinquency Prevention Act to broaden and integrate existing federal programs to deter juvenile delinquency. The act required the Law Enforcement Assistance Administration (LEAA) to establish and implement goals for existing juvenile delinquency programs. It also authorized LEAA to provide matching grants to local and private agencies to establish facilities and programs for runaway youth.

Four years later Hawkins was floor manager for a bill to extend the Comprehensive Employment and Training Act (CETA) that faced

*Hawkins addresses the Congressional Black Caucus in 1975.*

mounting criticism of its job training and public employment programs. The bill which passed that year resulted in the creation of 660,000 jobs. In 1984, as chairman of the Subcommittee on Employment Opportunities, he tried to steer passage of his proposal to curb the alarming rate of youth unemployment. His bill would have provided two billion dollars for full-time summer jobs and part-time jobs during the school year for disadvantaged youth who agreed to maintain performance standards and to remain in or return to school.

Education and jobs were closely related in Hawkins's thinking. In order for young people to succeed, they need the skills to make a contribution to society. Education, whether in schools or in job training programs, is the key to acquiring those skills. Society as a whole benefits, Hawkins believes, because job training and education programs pay off in the long run in tax-paying workers and higher tax revenues. Hawkins argues that it costs the economy billions of dollars each year because some 35 million Americans, many of whom are in the work force, are functionally illiterate.

Hawkins also supported domestic issues such as abortion funding, the creation of a consumer protection agency, the food stamp program and restrictions on strip mining. The Pregnancy Disability Act of 1978, sponsored by Hawkins, vastly expanded the rights of working women. This landmark legislation barred employers from discriminating on the basis of pregnancy and required them to cover pregnant workers in disability and health insurance plans. In defense and foreign affairs issues, he opposed controversial weapons systems such as the Safeguard Anti-Ballistic Missile, the MX missile and nuclear aircraft carriers, but he did vote for the B-1 Bomber in 1975.

## Retirement and Well-Deserved Honors

After over two decades in Congress, Gus decided to retire in 1991. Several factors influenced his decision. Ten years of contending with Republican Presidents, the huge sums of money needed to run for office and the fact that he was now well into his eighties required too much energy for him to carry out his responsibilities. The Congressional farewell ceremony took place in the Education and Labor Committee where his portrait as chairman was unveiled by his wife Elsie.

Augustus F. Hawkins deserves to be considered an outstanding Member of Congress because of his dedicated and skilled use of the legislative process to promote the values he believes are at the very core of a great society: the protection and education of the young, the poor and the infirmed; and the efforts to provide jobs for all working men and women. These are the principles by which he lived and which he believes are the values of the nation whose Constitution guarantees the pursuit of happiness and the general welfare of its people.

**For Further Reading:**

William Clay, *Just Permanent Interests: Black Americans in Congress, 1870-1992*, (1993).
Hans J. Massaquoi, "Gus Hawkins—Fifth Negro Congressman," *Ebony* (1963): 38-42.
Jacqueline Trescott, "The Long Haul of Rep. Gus Hawkins," *Washington Post*, 24 October 1990.

(Courtesy, Congressional Black Caucus, photo by Keith Jewell)

*Congressional Black Caucus poses on the House steps of the Capitol in 1977.
From left to right: (front row) Barbara Jordan, Robert Nix, Ralph Metcalfe,
Cardiss Collins, Parren Mitchell, Hawkins, Shirley Chisholm; (middle row)
John Conyers, Charles Rangel, Harold Ford, Yvonne Brathwaite Burke, Walter
Fauntroy; (back row) Ronald Dellums, Louis Stokes and Charles Diggs.*

The first generation of African-American leaders after the abolition of slavery strove to secure the promise of American politics—liberty and justice for all. Of the eleven men pictured on this 1883 poster, four are Members of Congress: Robert B. Elliot (top left), Blanche K. Bruce (top right), John M. Langston (bottom left) and Joseph H. Rainey (bottom right). Also pictured are Frederick Douglass (center) and clockwise from top center: William Wells Brown, Professor R.T. Greener, Reverend Richard Allen, Rainey, E.D. Bassett, Langston, P.B.S. Pinchback and Henry H. Garnett.

(U.S. Capitol Historical Society)

*After George Henry White of North Carolina left the House of Representatives in 1901, no African American was elected to Congress until 1928. When White left, he predicted that African Americans would return "phoenix-like." The election of Oscar De Priest in 1928 heralded the return. This political cartoon in the* Chicago Defender, *May 18, 1929, offered De Priest's election as a "history lesson" to African-American youth.*

William H. Gray (left), the most powerful African American Member of Congress when he retired in 1991 to direct the United Negro College Fund, passes the mantle of leadership to Kweisi Mfume (right), chairman of the Congressional Black Caucus. The journey of African Americans in Congress from Rainey and Revells to Gray and Mfume has been a shared experience uniting generations in the ceaseless quest to fulfill the American promise.

(Courtesy of William H. Gray)

# *Barbara Charline Jordan*

*(February 21, 1936-January 17, 1996)*
*Democrat-Texas (18th District)*
*93d-95th Congresses (1973-1979)*

## Defender of the Constitution

(Library of Congress)

*Congresswoman Barbara Jordan.*

Barbara Charline Jordan made history by becoming the first African American since 1883 to be elected to the Texas State Senate; the first African American to be elected president pro tempore (temporary presiding officer) of the Texas State Senate; the first and only African-American woman to be governor of a state (she was named governor for a day in Texas on June 10, 1972); and, most significantly, the first African-American woman from the South to be elected to the United States House of Representatives.

During her three terms in Congress (1973-1979), Barbara Jordan managed to convey to the whole nation her deep respect for the law and the Constitution. During the Watergate proceedings, her deep and impressive voice captivated the imagination of millions of Americans across the airwaves as she spoke eloquently about the single most important instrument that holds Americans together: the Constitution of the United States.

## Background

Barbara Charline Jordan was born on February 21, 1936, in Houston, Texas, the youngest of three daughters of Benjamin M. and Arlyne Jordan. Her father graduated from Tuskeegee Institute and worked at the Houston Terminal Warehouse and Cold Storage Company before beginning his Baptist ministry in 1949 at the Good Hope Missionary Baptist Church. Her father had a profound influence on her. Not only was she a faithful member of his church, but she also inherited his fierce ambition. He was a strict disciplinarian who chastised his daughter when she brought home anything lower than an "A" on her report card. As a result, Barbara Jordan never wanted to be an average person, she always wanted to excel.

Jordan graduated from Phyllis Wheatley High School in Houston in 1952 in the top five percent of her class. Her first career goal was to become a pharmacist. After hearing a speech at the high school's career day by Edith Sampson, a black lawyer from Chicago, she decided to become a lawyer. To that end, she studied political science and history at Texas Southern University, from which she graduated magna cum laude in 1956. She earned a bachelor of laws degree at Boston University in 1959; the following year she was admitted to the bar in Massachusetts and Texas.

Jordan returned to Houston in 1960, moved in with her parents and began practicing general civil law on the dining room table until she eventually scraped up enough money to open her own office three years later. She also worked as an Administrative Assistant to County Judge Bill Elliot in Harris County, Texas.

During the 1960 presidential campaign, Jordan directed Houston's first black "one person-per-block" precinct effort to drum up support for the Democratic ticket headed by nominees John F. Kennedy and Lyndon B. Johnson. In 1962 and 1964 she was an unsuccessful candidate for the state legislature.

## In the Texas Legislature

When Jordan was elected to the Texas State Senate in 1966, she took her seat alongside 30 white male colleagues. She was anxious to earn the respect of her peers as a serious legislator. President Lyndon Johnson, a fellow Democrat and Texan, recognized Barbara Jordan's talent soon after she won the election. He conferred with her in the White House over such matters as fair housing legislation. They remained friends for life.

Known throughout her career as a champion of the underprivileged, Jordan began her legislative program by supporting many of the causes that would later distinguish her Congressional career. While in the Texas Senate she was chair of the Labor and Management Relations Committee and vice chair of the Legislative, Congressional and Judicial committees. She steered a bill through the Senate that established the Fair Employment Practices Commission, fought for the passage of the state's first minimum wage laws and helped to create the state's Special Department of Community Affairs to deal with the problems of the state's urban areas. The highlight of her tenure came in 1972, when she was elected president pro-tempore of the Texas Senate. It was an important and symbolic achievement for a black legislator.

As a result of the population shifts shown by the 1970 census, Texas was awarded an additional seat (its 24th) in the United States

(Library of Congress)

*Jordan and members of the House Judiciary Committee open debate on impeachment of President Richard M. Nixon in 1974.*

Congress. The newly-drawn 18th Congressional District of Texas was 50-percent black and 15-percent Hispanic. This information persuaded Jordan to enter the district Democratic primary in 1972 against Curtis Graves, another black state legislator. Graves attacked her for having close ties to the establishment and called her an "Uncle Tom." She ignored the charges and ran a positive campaign in which she captured 80 percent of the vote in the primary and went on to trounce Republican Paul Merritt in the general election with a plurality of 66,000 votes out of 85,000 votes cast.

## Congressional Career

On January 3, 1973, Barbara Jordan was sworn in and took her seat as the first African-American Member of Congress from Texas since the Reconstruction era. In fact, she and her fellow freshman colleague in the 93d Congress, Andrew Young of Georgia, were the first African Americans elected to Congress from the South since 1898. Her committee assignments included the House Judiciary Committee, the Committee on Government Operations and the Steering and Policy Committee of the House Democratic Caucus.

Congresswoman Jordan's liberal legislative agenda consistently supported efforts to raise the standard of living of impoverished Americans. She backed programs of the Office of Economic Opportunity which provided services to the poor such as the establishment of an independent public corporation to provide free legal services to the poor and the creation of the Consumer Protection Agency.

As a member of the Judiciary Committee, which oversaw the impeachment hearings of President Richard Nixon, Jordan made her most dramatic appearance speaking eloquently in defense of the United States Constitution. The 1974 hearings grew out of the Watergate affair when five men linked to the Republican Committee for the Reelection of the President were caught illegally wiretapping the Democratic national headquarters. After the President was implicated in a conspiracy to cover up the affair, the House Judiciary Committee convened hearings on May 9, 1974, to consider impeachment proceedings. Congresswoman Jordan concluded the crisis was a test of the Constitution—a challenge to the legislative branch's obligation to hold the executive branch responsible to the law.

When Jordan spoke at the Watergate hearings, it was with a note of irony as well as fervor that all African American Congressional legislators must sometimes feel. In her own words, Barbara Jordan mused: "'We the people'—it is a very eloquent beginning. But when the Constitution of the United States was completed on the seventeenth of September in 1787, I was not included in that 'We the people.' I felt for many years that somehow George Washington and Alexander Hamilton just left me out by mistake. But through the process of amendment, interpretation, and court decision, I have finally been included in 'We the people.' Today I am an inquisitor. I believe hyperbole would not be fictional and would not overstate the solemnness that I feel right now. My faith in the Constitution is whole. It is complete. It is total. I am not going to sit here and be an idle spectator to the diminution, the subversion, the destruction of the Constitution."

President Nixon chose to resign rather than face impeachment. His successor, President Gerald Ford, asked Jordan to be one of his personal representatives to Peking, China, in 1974.

As a Member of Congress, Jordan concentrated her efforts on domestic affairs. Elements of her legislative agenda included helping to pass the Consumer Goods Pricing Act of 1975. She supported legislation that created federally-funded programs for the treatment and prevention of diabetes, cancer and alcoholism. She endorsed the creation of a National Institute on Aging and the expansion of a program to guarantee nutritionally-balanced meals. She advocated increased federal aid to cities and recommended direct grants from the Law Enforcement Assistance Administration to metropolitan police departments and subsidies for the operations of urban mass transit systems. She worked for the repeal of federal authorization for state Fair Trade Laws which sanctioned certain price-fixing schemes.

An outspoken critic of large military expenditures, Jordan voted to reduce the number of American troops stationed abroad to impose a ceiling on military aid to South Vietnam and to override President Nixon's veto of the War Powers Act limiting the president's authority to commit American troops overseas.

At the Democratic National Convention in July 1976, Jordan became the first African-American woman to deliver the keynote address of a major political party. She made a powerful impression with her rich speaking voice. She was again asked to give the keynote speech at the Party Convention of 1992 to an aroused, receptive audience.

## A Busy Retirement

On December 10, 1977, Jordan announced that she would not be a candidate for reelection in 1978. It was a stunning and unexpected retirement. She was a popular Member of Congress and her premature departure set off many rumors. She explained that she had done all she wanted to do in Congress and wished to return to her native state and do other things.

Whatever her reasons for retiring from Congress, in 1978 she went on to become a professor with an endowed chair teaching public policy and political ethics at the Lyndon B. Johnson School of Public Affairs at the University of Texas in Austin. From 1979 to 1981 she served on President Carter's Advisory Board on Ambassadorial Appointments. In 1991 Jordan was appointed special counsel on ethics to Governor Ann Richards of Texas. She also served on a United Nations panel that examined the role of international corporations operating in South Africa and Namibia.

Barbara Jordan never married nor had children, but she was loved and revered by her students. President Clinton appointed her to chair the United States Commission on Immigration Reform, a bipartisan group that submitted its recommendations on immigration reform to the President in September 1994. For the last several years of her life she was confined to a wheelchair and walker by multiple sclerosis. She died on January 17, 1996, at a hospital in Austin from pneumonia and complications of leukemia.

## Honors and Awards

Barbara Jordan began her illustrious career as a legislator with a bang. She was named the outstanding freshman of the year in the Texas Senate.

*(Houston Chronicle)*

*Former President Lyndon B. Johnson and Jordan on the campaign trail.*

By 1977 she had already been awarded 22 honorary doctoral degrees bestowed by various colleges and universities. She considered the honorary degree from Harvard University to be the highlight of such honors because earlier in her life she had been discouraged from applying to that prestigious institution's law school. Harvard not only gave her an honorary doctorate, but also asked her to give the commencement address at the same ceremony. In 1984 she received the Eleanor Roosevelt Award from the International Platform Association, which had admitted her as a member of its Orators Hall of Fame and deemed her the "Best Living Orator." She also helped to found People For the American Way. In 1990 Barbara Jordan was inducted into the National Women's Hall of Fame in Seneca Falls, New York.

Representative Barbara Jordan was an outstanding Member of Congress. Though her tenure in the institution was brief, she proved to be a formidable legislator. She was a superb role model for all young people. Current D.C. Delegate Eleanor Holmes Norton observed, "There is no black woman in politics today that is not in her debt." She had a powerful presence. She could spellbind an audience with what the veteran political observer Theodore H. White once described as "a flow of Churchillian eloquence, of resonance, boom and grip so compelling as to make one forget to take notes." America was fortunate to have had such an eloquent defender of the Constitution in Congress at a time of national pain.

(Ap/Wide World Photos)

*Jordan delivers the keynote address at the 1992 Democratic National Convention in New York City.*

**For Further Reading:**

Ira B. Bryant, *Barbara Charline Jordan: From the Ghetto to the Capitol*, (1977).
James Haskins, *Barbara Jordan*, (1977).
Barbara Jordan and Shelby Hearon, *Barbara Jordan: A Self-Portrait*, (1979).
Maurice Roberts, *Barbara Jordan: The Great Lady From Texas*, (1984).

# George Thomas "Mickey" Leland

*(November 27, 1944-August 7, 1989)*
*Democrat-Texas (18th District)*
*96th-101st Congresses (1979-89)*

## Anti-Hunger Crusader

(AP/Wide World Photos)

*Congressman Mickey Leland.*

George Thomas "Mickey" Leland came to Congress with the enthusiasm of a dedicated reformer seeking to address important social issues on a global scale. He sought to connect problems of hunger and poverty in the United States with those of the Third World, especially Africa. Much of his legislative agenda was devoted to refocusing American foreign policy away from the east-west Cold War mentality to concentrate more on the relationship between rich and poor nations.

The subsequent collapse of the Soviet Union and the end of the Cold War seemed to reinforce his point of view. Ironically, Congressman Leland died in an airplane crash in Africa on a mission of mercy the same year as the momentous events which brought the end of Soviet totalitarianism. Mickey died as he had lived—a humanitarian trying to feed the desperately hungry and to redirect his nation's foreign policy priorities.

## Childhood and Education

George Thomas Leland was born on November 27, 1944, in Lubbock, Texas. "Mickey," the nickname his grandfather gave him, stuck with him for the rest of his life, both personally and professionally. His parents separated soon after his birth. Mickey's mother, Alice Rains, moved her young family to an impoverished neighborhood in Houston's Fifth Ward. Besides being a single mother, Alice worked as a short-order cook while putting herself through school to become a teacher. She was a courageous, strong-willed woman who greatly influenced her sons, Mickey and Gaston.

Leland was an excellent student and graduated from Phyllis Wheatley High School in 1963. He enrolled as a premed student in Texas Southern University in Houston. He graduated in 1970 with a bachelor of science degree in pharmacy. After graduation he remained at Texas Southern as an instructor in Clinical Pharmacy (1970-71).

The poverty in which he was born and raised provided Leland with personal insights into the problems of the poor and hungry. His devout Roman Catholic faith further strengthened his sympathy for the disadvantaged. As a young man in the 1960s he was deeply influenced by the winds of change blowing in that decade.

Imbued with youthful idealism, bright young people such as Mickey Leland believed they could change the world for the better. Like many young African Americans attending college in the 1960s, he was exposed to the writings of Malcolm X, Amiri Baraka and Julius Nyerere, former Tanzanian president, all of whom urged African Americans to be more active in working to remedy the problems of their people.

A turning point in Leland's life came when he was arrested in a protest against police brutality. His life had reached a crossroads. As a self-proclaimed radical, he could have chosen to fight injustice and suffering outside of the system; but he realized that it would be more constructive to work for change within the law.

As a student at Texas Southern University, Leland began to work with the Medical Committee for Human Rights, a group of health professionals who established free health clinics, and the Black Panther Party, a militant political group. He later went on to form a group called the Black Community Action Team. He was a director of special development projects at Hermann Hospital in Houston from 1971 to 1978.

## A Startling Appearance in the Texas Legislature

Leland first ran for public office in 1972 when he was elected to the Texas State Legislature. Serving in that body from 1973 to 1978, he championed health issues and showed that minorities in Texas were an up-and-coming political force. Active in Democratic Party politics, he became a member of the Democratic National Committee (DNC) from 1976 to 1981.

Leland's initial appearance in the Texas Legislature startled his conservative colleagues when he strode in wearing a big Afro hairstyle, platform shoes, a leather shoulder bag and a colorful tie-died dashiki (African shirt—the fashionable look of a young militant of the time. He made his first trip to Africa shortly after his election. He immediately fell in love with the continent. His scheduled three-week visit to Tanzania lasted for three months as he absorbed the culture and developed a strong attachment to the people.

(AP/Wide World Photos)

*Speaker Tip O'Neill swears Leland into office in 1979.*

## Fighting against World Hunger in the U.S. Congress

When Representative Barbara Jordan (D-TX) announced her retirement in 1978, Leland decided to take on the challenge of national politics. Encouraged and supported by John de Menil, a Houston human rights activist and philanthropist, Leland defeated two well-established opponents to win election to the 96th Congress.

Leland entered the United States House of Representatives in January 1979. For the next ten years he represented the 18th District of Texas, which included the Fifth Ward of his childhood. The district's racial composition was 39-percent African American, 27-percent Hispanic and 34-percent white. He became fluent in Spanish. Once during the Voting Rights Act extension debate he stunned his colleagues by arguing for the preservation of the law's bilingual clauses by speaking in Spanish on the floor of the House.

From 1981 to 1985, Leland chaired the Democratic National Committee's Black Caucus. He surprised many of his colleagues by actively supporting Walter Mondale's candidacy over Jesse Jackson's quest for the Democratic presidential nomination in 1984. However, he

(AP/Wide World Photos)

*Congressman Leland chaired the House Select Committee on Hunger.*

did become a top fundraiser for the Jackson candidacy in the 1988 primary campaign.

During his ten years in Congress, Leland held a variety of committee assignments. He was a member of the Committee on Energy and Commerce and its Energy and Power, Health and the Environment, Consumer Protection, and Telecommunications and Finance Subcommittees. He took an active role in demanding higher hiring percentages for women and minorities in the telecommunications industry. He was known for arguing with television executives for more diverse off-camera employment and improved minority role model images on screen. In 1984 he authored the equal employment opportunity language in the Cable Act that called for more minority ownership. Other committee assignments included the Post Office and Civil Service Committee and its Subcommittees on Compensation and Employee Benefits and Postal Operations and Services, the later of which he chaired.

In spite of his many Congressional achievements, Leland will always be best remembered for his efforts to end hunger through his role in the creation of the 16-member House Select Committee on Hunger which he chaired. Shortly after he entered Congress in 1979, Leland began pushing for a House committee on hunger. He encountered criticism from some Members who argued that creating another committee would waste time and money and infringe on already existing committees. Through patient coalition building and tireless persuasion over a five-year period, Congressman Leland succeeded in getting the select committee appointed.

The committee's first job was to determine the worldwide extent of the hunger problem. This included conducting surveys of the problems of domestic and international hunger and malnutrition. While serving as Chairman of the House Select Committee on Hunger, he helped boost American assistance to famine-stricken victims in the Sudan and Ethiopia. In 1984, his committee obtained 800 million dollars of famine relief for Africa at a time when the world had become aware of the extent of the problem through heart-rending television coverage and the fundraising efforts of musical artists in the United States and Great Britain.

Chairman Leland also strongly advocated the adoption of U.S. sanctions against South Africa until that nation discarded its policy of racial discrimination known as apartheid. He chaired the Congressional Black Caucus (CBC) from 1985 to 1986, a period in which its members became intensely engaged in bringing an end to apartheid. In collaboration with TransAfrica, an African-American lobby, the CBC advocated trade sanctions and participated in civil disobedience protests in front of the South African Embassy in Washington, D.C. The Anti-Apartheid Act of 1986 was the culmination of a broad coalition of forces in Congress led by members of the CBC.

Leland had other humanitarian interests. He was an occasional emissary for the State Department to Cuba because he had developed a working relationship with Cuban President Fidel Castro, whom he visited about a dozen times and with whom he could communicate directly in Spanish. While disagreeing profoundly with the Cuban dictator's ideology, he did respect Castro for his intellect and his political influence in the Third World. Moreover, Leland negotiated the release of three Cuban political prisoners and their families. Likewise, when he went to Hanoi, he was able to negotiate the exodus of three children whose fathers had fled Vietnam. Soon after Leland won his first Congressional election, he founded a program to send African-American teenagers from Houston to Israel for six weeks to learn about Jewish culture and heritage. He once bicycled across Israel and was a great supporter of that nation's right to exist.

**Marriage and Fatherhood**

Leland met Alison Walton, then a 24 year-old Georgetown University law student at the annual Congressional Black Caucus weekend in 1982. They married in 1983. She eventually became an investment banker. The high point of their marriage was the birth of their first son, Jarrett David, which had a profound impact upon Leland's already heightened concern for young people. He once exclaimed, "I have always wanted to be a father." Fatherhood enhanced his attention to the issues of hunger and world peace and his determination to make the world better for children. Sadly, in trying to save others, especially children, he was deprived of raising his twin boys, Cameron George and Austin Mickey, who were born just months after his death. Jarrett David was only three when his father left on his last fateful African trip in 1989.

Although Leland was certainly an idealist and humanitarian, he was also realistic about the nature of Africa's internal conflicts. He often had long talks with Mengistu, then military leader of Ethiopia, where much of his effort was centered. Mengistu's government had poor relations with the United States; yet Leland's focus was singlemindedly on getting relief to the innocent victims of internal disorder.

Leland was once interviewed on the television program "Nightline" and honestly assessed the endless disasters in Africa as being as much man-made as natural. Nevertheless, his chief concern was the survival of the innocent human victims of war and famine. When Congressman Leland's plane disappeared in the forests and mountains of Ethiopia on August 7, 1989, Mengistu quickly gave permission for American military planes to join the search for survivors. The world mourned when it was learned that Leland had lost his life on a humanitarian mission to feed the starving people of Africa.

Congressman Leland often related the source of his sustained interest in humanitarian relief for the starving victims of hunger in Africa. During a visit to a refugee camp in the Horn of Africa, he had held a starving child in his arms. The child looked him in the eye. Leland momentarily turned away to ask about her condition; but when he looked back, she had died. The experience had a deep and lasting effect upon him. Because of her, Congressman Leland was responsible for saving thousands of other children from starvation.

Members of Congress, especially his colleagues in the Congressional Black Caucus, felt a deep sense of loss with the death of Mickey Leland. The CBC renamed its humanitarian award in his memory in 1989. Leland's life and works were widely eulogized throughout the world. In Houston, the largest terminal at the airport was renamed the Mickey Leland International Airlines Building in his honor. President George Bush spoke for many Americans when he connected Leland's humanitarian concerns in the United States and Africa: " [Congressman Leland] was engaged in a noble cause—trying to feed the hungry. . . . His sense of compassion and desire to help those in need has aided millions of people from Houston to Addis Ababa."

*Leland loads sacks of food and supplies during his relief mission to Africa in
1989. He was killed when the plane crashed in the rugged mountains of
Ethiopia.*

**For Further Reading:**

William L. Clay, *Just Permanent Interests: Black Americans in Congress, 1870-1992,* (1993).
Mickey Leland, "Toward a National Policy to End Homelessness,"
*America,* January 31, 1987, pp. 69-71.
Mickey Leland, "What African-Americans Can Do About Starvation in Africa,"
*Ebony* (October 1989): 80-84.

# Parren James Mitchell

*(April 29, 1922-)*
*Democrat-Maryland (Seventh District)*
*92d-99th Congresses (1971-1987)*

## Affirmative Action Activist

(Library of Congress)

*Congressman Parren Mitchell.*

**P**arren J. Mitchell, the first African American elected to Congress from Maryland, earned a reputation as a vigorous advocate of minority participation in small business ownership and affirmative action programs. As a Member of Congress he sponsored legislation to provide equal access and assistance to economically disadvantaged groups that historically had been excluded from the American dream.

### The Mitchells of Maryland: From Poverty to Prominence

Born in Baltimore on April 29, 1922, Parren was one of ten children of Clarence M. Mitchell, Sr., a waiter, and Elsie Davis Mitchell. This family of modest means has come to occupy a position of prominence in Maryland politics that mirrors much of the success of the civil rights movement—racial progress achieved through activism within the legal and political system.

The family's roots reach back to rural Mississippi. Like many poor African-American families in the South, the Mitchells migrated north in the early decades of the twentieth century to escape poverty only to encounter rigid racial segregation in northern cities. After settling in Baltimore, the family provided "P.J." (his family nickname) and his brothers a solid childhood environment that was close-knit, supportive, hard-working and church-going, in spite of the hardships of the Great Depression of the late 1920s and '30s.

Parren's older brother, Clarence, was always his hero. As a young man, Clarence Mitchell was a reporter for the *Afro-American*, a prominent African-American newspaper in Baltimore. He spent the rest of his life as a Washington lobbyist for the National Association for the Advancement of Colored People (NAACP). Clarence's son, Clarence Mitchell III, later became well-known as a flamboyant state senator who ran for mayor of Baltimore. Parren's sister-in-law, Juanita Jackson Mitchell, became president of the state chapter of the NAACP and a prominent lawyer.

### Education and Civic Activism

Parren Mitchell graduated from Baltimore's Douglass High School in 1940. He entered the U.S. Army in 1942 as a commissioned officer and

company commander of the all-black 92d Infantry Division. (The Armed
Forces were not integrated until after an executive order issued by
President Truman in 1948). Mitchell won a Purple Heart when he was
seriously wounded during combat in Italy, and was honorably discharged
in 1946 after the end of World War II.

Educational benefits provided by the 1944 GI Bill of Rights permitted Mitchell to attend Morgan State College, an historically black
institution of higher education in Baltimore, from which he graduated in
1950 with a B.A. degree.

The decade of the 1950s was pivotal for race relations in education and public accommodations in the United States. The NAACP
became the leading organization to challenge discrimination through
legal action. A brilliant lawyer, Thurgood Marshall, who argued the landmark 1954 *Brown* v. *Board of Education* case that prohibited racial segregation in public schools, and who later became a Supreme Court justice, helped Mitchell become the first black graduate student at the
College Park campus of the University of Maryland in 1950. He graduated in 1952 with a master's degree in sociology. Mitchell then returned to
Morgan State as a sociology instructor (1953-1954).

Putting his education to practical use, Mitchell became a
Baltimore probation officer from 1954 to 1957. The experience made a

(AP/Wide World Photos)

*In 1970 Mitchell, a 48-year old sociology professor at Morgan State University,
became the first African American elected to Congress from Maryland.*

lasting impression and alerted him to the uneven application of justice to inner city youth and poor people. In the next few years he went through a variety of jobs, some paid and some volunteer, while still taking graduate courses in sociology.

In May of 1963, Mitchell was named executive secretary of the Maryland Commission on Interracial Problems and Relations. The commission implemented the public accommodations law and administered the state's Fair Employment Practices Law.

President Lyndon Johnson's War on Poverty afforded Mitchell the chance to lead his city's efforts as director of the Baltimore Community Action Agency from 1965 to 1968. As a community activist and a member of a family with growing political prominence, he had sought solutions to segregation and economic inequality in the private sector. Politics had only become important to him due to his interest in poverty issues. While he did appreciate President Johnson's antipoverty program, like many members of his generation, he had been politicized by the civil rights movement which was in full swing by the 1960s and the anti-Vietnam War movement which was reaching its zenith in 1968. As an antipoverty activist, he lamented the war as a wasteful diversion of resources and energy from pressing domestic needs.

## First African American Elected to Congress from Maryland

Parren Mitchell had not considered running for public office until persuaded to do so by a number of community groups. No African American had ever been elected to the U.S. Congress from Maryland. Moreover, he had not been on good terms with local Democratic Party leaders who viewed him as a militant supported by the radical Black Panther Party. Ironically, Mitchell did have good relations with the moderate Republican mayor, and he was popular in the African-American community and with white liberals. He made an unsuccessful run for Congress in the 1968 Democratic primary against an 18-year incumbent, but he won a rematch in 1970 and defeated his Republican opponent in the general election. The campaign was not without violence; his headquarters were fire-bombed but no one was injured.

Mitchell entered the 92d Congress in January 1971 and served through the 99th Congress (1985-1987). A strident opponent of the Vietnam War before he entered Congress, Mitchell and two colleagues went to court to have the war declared unconstitutional. A year later, he joined 23 fellow Members of Congress in a lawsuit to halt the bombing and mining of North Vietnamese ports. He consistently condemned the war and openly chastised other Members for not doing the same.

## Learning Patience and Gaining Expertise

As a freshman Member of Congress and as an urban black liberal Democrat, Mitchell found it difficult to influence legislation. Freshmen Members have historically had to wait their turn, but it is a difficult lesson to learn.

Mitchell became a frustrated, chain-smoking workaholic who averaged 14-hour workdays. He believed the poor had few advocates in Congress, and he was dedicated to advancing their cause. He stayed in touch with his constituents by listing his telephone number in the local directory. Each day he commuted the 40 miles between his Capitol Hill office and his restored bachelor's inner city townhouse in Baltimore.

It was not until his fourth term that Mitchell's influence grew more important as people both inside and outside of Congress began to seek his opinions. He enthusiastically supported the Humphrey-Hawkins Full Employment Act of 1976 as the key to a successful urban policy. He pressed for increased spending on federal jobs programs, minority-owned small businesses and reduced defense spending.

Mitchell's committee assignments included membership on the following committees: the House Budget Committee; the Small Business Committee and chairmanship of its Task Force on Minority Enterprise; the Banking, Finance and Urban Affairs Committee and chairmanship of its Subcommittee on Domestic Monetary Policy and membership on the Housing and Community Development Subcommittee. In 1981 he became chairman of the House Small Business Committee in the 97th Congress and vice-chairman of the Joint Committee on Defense Production.

In 1977 Mitchell became chairman of the Congressional Black Caucus (CBC), which had 16 members at the time. He also chaired its Subcommittee on Housing, Minority Enterprise and Economic Development. He became the first African American to hold a leadership position in Congress when his fellow Democrats elected him one of eleven whips-at-large. He was also named to the Presidential Commission on the National Agenda for the 1980s.

## Mitchell's Affirmative Action Philosophy

Much of Congressman Mitchell's work on behalf of minorities and minority-owned businesses was based on the concept of affirmative action. Although critics have equated it with a quota system, its proponents saw affirmative action as a way to permit minority individuals and minority-owned businesses to share in American economic development by setting goals in hiring and the awarding of government contracts.

Mitchell considered his greatest legislative achievements to be his amendments to promote the participation of minorities in American business. He attached the Mitchell amendment to the four-billion-dollar Local Public Works Capital Development and Investment Act of 1976, which compelled state, county and municipal governments seeking federal grants to set aside ten percent of those grants for minority-owned firms. The law was upheld by the Supreme Court in 1980.

Mitchell sponsored the Small Business Act Amendment of 1977 to require federal agencies to increase procurement opportunities for disadvantaged businesses and obligated those agencies to set goals for awarding contracts to minority subcontractors. Provisions of the law allowed the Small Business Administration (SBA) to impose a moratorium on loan repayment in bad economic times.

Mitchell was a strong supporter of the Small Business Administration. He opposed efforts to increase interest rates for loans to small businesses and to reduce SBA disaster loans. He also opposed efforts to enact a sub-minimum wage for workers under the age of 18.

Philosophically, Congressman Mitchell was as much a social crusader as he was a politician. His sense of social justice dictated his politics. He viewed economic parity between the races as essential to a just society. He acknowledged that minorities had gained some upward social mobility through school desegregation, equal access to public accommo-

*Mitchell chaired the Congressional Black Caucus from 1977 to 1979. Here he introduces his successor, Congresswoman Cardiss Collins.*

dations and voting rights legislation; but he did not see these achievements bringing the economic progress which he regarded as the key to real equality.

Racial barriers had prevented open access to the free enterprise system for minorities. Politics, Mitchell believed, should be used to level the playing field. Affirmative action and the Mitchell amendments were Congressional devices to insure that minorities got their fair share of a market that otherwise would not voluntarily be open to them. Set-asides and other requirements, he argued, simply facilitated that part of the Constitution which obligated Congress to promote the general welfare. "Our government has subsidized airlines, farmers, oil industries. . . . I maintain that the federal government has the duty, the responsibility and the obligation to subsidize Black enterprise," he stated in the 1970s.

Mitchell viewed the election of President Ronald Reagan as a setback for affirmative action. During the Reagan presidency, he lamented the actions of the Justice Department and the Supreme Court as those institutions became dominated by opponents of affirmative action.

### An Activist in Retirement

Even though disappointed with national political developments, Mitchell has remained active even in retirement. He decided not to run for reelection in 1986, but he did run unsuccessfully for the Democratic nomination for lieutenant governor of Maryland.

In 1986, he founded the Minority Business Legal Defense and Education Fund, a private organization that acts as a national advocate and legal representative for the minority business community. He has been credited with mentoring hundreds of young African-American professionals on business techniques. He continues to be an active force in the organization as a means to promote the primary interests of his public life.

Congressman Mitchell has written several monographs and co-authored *Signal Four-Family Trouble*. He has received numerous honorary degrees, more than 150 awards and many citations from educational institutions and civic organizations. The citation that accompanied his honorary doctor of laws degree from Lincoln University in Pennsylvania read in part: ". . . this son and servant of the Seventh Congressional District of Maryland, and of the nation, has been a creative craftsman and an impassioned artisan in pursuit of goals of liberty, justice, and equality for all Americans." This sentiment was mirrored by his colleagues in the Congressional Black Caucus.

In spite of his early frustrations, Parren Mitchell was able to become one of the most effective Congressional advocates of affirmative action and the development of minority-owned small businesses. He turned his frustrations as an activist into positive results through the acquisition of experience and expertise. Time and experience earned him respect. A colleague, Representative Butler Derrick (D-SC), noted, "He . . . moved to a position of influence, based on his skills and expertise. He's become a leader across the board, especially in economic policy."

**For Further Reading:**

*A Salute to a Living Legend!* (1993, published by the Minority Business Enterprise Legal Defense and Education Fund)
William L. Clay, *Just Permanent Interests: Black Americans in Congress, 1870-1992*, (1993).
Parren J. Mitchell, "What Went Wrong with the Dream?" *Engage/ Social Action Journal* (1979): 9-40.

# Adam Clayton Powell, Jr.

*(November 29, 1908-April 4, 1972)*
*Democrat-New York (22d and 18th Districts)*
*79th-89th, 91st Congresses (1945-67, 1969-71)*

## Mr. Civil Rights

When Adam Clayton Powell, Jr., took his seat in Congress on January 3, 1945, the only other African American in Congress was William Dawson, the quiet and diligent representative from Chicago. Powell entered Congress with a mission to make his mark on the institution. From his seat in Congress, he wanted to fight racial discrimination in public facilities while advancing the political and economic status of blacks. At the same time, he had an unyielding dedication to bring an end to poverty for all citizens, black and white.

## Harlem Roots

Adam Clayton Powell, Jr., loved politics. Although he was a Democrat by affiliation, he considered himself an independent spirit. The quintessential Harlem Renaissance man was flamboyant, handsome, dapper, confident and articulate with a singular focus on civil rights. His major weakness perhaps was that of being a bon vivant, or having a penchant for the good life. But, if so, he came by it honestly. By the time he was born, his father had attained prominence as pastor of a prosperous church in New Haven, Connecticut. Consequently, young Powell was raised in an unusually comfortable home in a racially integrated environment that few members of his race had ever known.

His father, however, began life as did most people of his race by growing up poor, segregated and uneducated in the South. Fortunately, the senior Adam Clayton Powell's rebellious nature, sense of adventure and just plain good luck propelled him out of the region. He found opportunities for work in the Midwest and the North and the chance to get a good secondary and college education. He wanted his son to have even greater opportunities.

Born on November 29, 1908, in New Haven, Connecticut, Adam Junior was the only son of his father and mother Mattie. After the family moved to New York City, young Adam was sent to a prestigious private school in the city and then attended City College. Although he had not been a serious student, he excelled after transferring to Colgate University in upstate New York. From then on, he committed himself to a life of acquiring knowledge, hard work and service that very much pleased his father. Not only did he graduate from Colgate University in 1930, but he also attended Union Theological Seminary and earned a master of arts degree in 1932 from Columbia University.

*Congressman Adam Clayton Powell.*

The bond between father and son grew stronger over the years. These bonds were tested when Adam Senior opposed his son's marriage to actress Isabel Washington in 1933 as inappropriate for a rising assistant pastor. Nevertheless, Adam Junior's strong self-confidence and speaking skills were acquired from his father's inspired sermons about the need for racial progress that he had heard as a child. These childhood experiences, no doubt, contributed to his decision to follow in his father's footsteps in the ministry. He was also shaped by the hardships of the Great Depression while he grew up. Although he did not personally experience deprivation, he developed a deep sympathy for those who did.

Powell's political moorings could be traced to the church his father founded in Harlem in 1923. The Abyssinian Baptist Church became the area's largest Baptist church. Powell later succeeded his father as pastor of the church from 1937 to 1971. It was a potential power base for the progressive politics to which he was attracted in early adulthood. The new black migrants from the South moving into previously white Harlem were the ultimate outsiders. Only those groups that favored reform, such as the progressives, offered the possibility of change that included outsiders. Powell, therefore, easily identified with them.

The Harlem Hospital case launched Powell's career as an activist. In 1925, five black doctors had been hired at the only hospital that treated the new arrivals in the city. This racial progress was turned to despair by the continued abysmal conditions that existed in the hospital called "the butcher shop." When the doctors publicly complained in 1933, they were dismissed. That act incensed Powell. When he confronted the local political bosses, he was treated in a condescending way, which further angered him. Powell, as an angry young man with great oratorical skills, displayed his ability to stir church members to action. He led some 1,500 protesters in a march on City Hall. Newspaper photographs of the event showed what came to be his leadership style—a handsome, young, impeccably dressed man with consternation on his face as he addressed an attentive crowd.

Powell's activism drew allies among reformers and progressives for his willingness to confront the local political bosses. In 1932, he launched a campaign against the stores along 125th Street, the main commercial corridor where blacks shopped but where they could not work. The dramatic picketing and marching did open up some jobs; but the courts subsequently ended the picketing. The strength of Adam Clayton Powell as a political activist, as viewed by friend and foe alike, provided the basis for his political career.

## The People's Voice in Congress

In 1941, New York created a new Congressional district for Harlem, but the seat would not become available until 1944. In 1942, Powell won a seat on the New York City Council by a landslide. He was sworn in by Mayor Fiorello La Guardia in January, not long after the United States entered World War II. Powell was concerned about building the morale of African-American troops in the segregated Armed Forces. He used the two-and-a-half-year period to expand his national reputation with an eye on the newly-created Congressional district by visiting bases and demanding equal treatment for black soldiers. He also began a weekly newspaper, the *People's Voice*, in support of his progressive views.

*Powell and supporters celebrate his victory in the 1958 Democratic primary.*

By the time Powell took his seat in the 79th Congress in January 1945, his national reputation had grown among the African-American population. After all, there were only two sitting African-American Members in the House and none in the Senate. Moreover, his bold, self-confident style quickly endeared him to many other Americans who felt oppressed.

Powell was always troubled by the discrepancy between the ideals of American democracy and the reality of American inequality. His uncompromising views often made his colleagues uncomfortable. In the segregated capital of the world's leading democracy, he found that in Congress, as in no other place, could one see the great disparities of American life. Powell knew why his new surroundings both pained and challenged him: "It was a place of timid souls, men bound by class, region, and party, . . . men who were quiet, so quiet that they eventually disappeared into anonymity."

Powell did not enter Congress quietly. He immediately clashed with one of the House's most influential Members, John E. Rankin of Mississippi, an arch-segregationist who was angered by the Harlem Congressman's audacity. Noting the humiliating treatment of black workers within the Capitol itself, Powell immediately challenged the institution's unwritten practices by regularly eating in the segregated dining room "reserved for Members of Congress only." Rankin was outraged that Powell not only used the facilities himself, but also brought members of his staff and friends to dine with him. Rankin vowed never to sit next to him. This stance goaded Powell to attempt to sit as close to

*Chairing the House Committee on Education and Labor from 1961-1967 was the highlight of Powell's Congressional career.*

Rankin as possible whenever he appeared on the House floor. The press noted that the Southern Congressman moved five times during a single day's session to avoid Powell. It was that disdain for prejudice that often got Powell into trouble. His style was confrontational, even menacing, when faced with the evils of racism.

Powell's initial Congressional assignments were with the Indian Affairs, Invalid Pensions and Labor Committees. These relatively low-profile assignments did not prevent him from introducing legislation that would outlaw lynching, abolish the poll tax and end racial discrimination in employment, housing, interstate transportation and the Armed Forces.

The assignment on the Committee on Education and Labor in 1947 was the heart of Powell's legislative career. The highlight of his tenure came as chairman of the committee from 1961 through 1967. Powell was at his most productive during this period, shepherding into law some 49 pieces of legislation that formed the backbone of the Johnson administration's War on Poverty.

His greatest legislative accomplishments included expanded educational opportunities, job training, minimum wage protection, school lunches and aid to elementary and secondary education. He consistently sought to deny federal funds to any enterprise that practiced racial discrimination by attaching a Powell amendment to a wide variety of legislation. At times, this tactic got him into trouble, such as the time a West Virginia Congressman punched him out during a dispute over a school construction bill. A version of the Powell amendment was incorporated as Title VI of the landmark Civil Rights Act of 1964.

Powell's leadership spanned a long and sometimes turbulent period of change not only in America but abroad as well. In many ways, he was ahead of his time. For example, he was one of the earliest Members of Congress to appreciate the powerful anticolonial forces in the Third World—forces he believed the United States should unequivocally support.

Powell attended the landmark 1955 Pan Asian-African Conference in Bandung, Indonesia, as an observer. In a press conference there, he defended the United States against charges leveled by Communist journalists that blacks in America were horribly mistreated. His stout defense was impressive. While acknowledging obvious discrimination, he pointed out that he was living proof that racism and second-class citizenship were on their way out. Moreover, in the closed sessions, he was able to weaken a Chinese-backed resolution condemning American racism. His performance was applauded by the *Herald Tribune*, the Hearst newspapers and received a citation from the Veterans of Foreign Wars.

After his Indonesian trip, Powell traveled in the South to support the bus boycott organized in Montgomery, Alabama, after Rosa Parks was arrested for not giving up her seat to a white passenger. Using his own New York experience, he provided strategic advice to the civil rights movement's emerging leader, the Reverend Martin Luther King, Jr. So endemic was overt racism at the time that the firestorm of criticism caused by Powell's meeting with the moderate governor of Alabama, Jim Folsom, helped ruin the governor's political career.

(Lyndon Baines Johnson Library)

*Powell confers with President Lyndon B. Johnson in the White House on July 21, 1966.*

## The Downward Spiral of a Brilliant Career

Some well-publicized missteps along the way led to Powell's downfall. He was a man of immense pride, a quality that can be both beneficial and detrimental. Given Powell's theatrical style, it contributed to the cloud of controversy hanging over the end of his Congressional career.

His string of marriages and divorces offended the traditional-minded. His second marriage in August 1945 to the beautiful pianist Hazel Scott produced his first son, Adam Clayton Powell III. After they were divorced in 1960, Powell married his third wife, Yvette Diago Flores, a secretary from Puerto Rico and mother of his second son, Adam Clayton Powell IV. The marriage ended in separation in 1965; but Powell kept her on his Congressional payroll even though she had returned to Puerto Rico.

A controversial lawsuit added to Powell's woes. To avoid paying the judgment or being served papers for contempt of court, Powell began a long exile from his district, only returning on Sundays when the papers could not be served.

Because Powell was such a highly visible public figure, his problems were magnified in the press. By 1967 his actions had outraged even some of his defenders in Congress. The House of Representatives voted to exclude Powell by a vote of 307 to 116. He was accused of being in criminal contempt of court and abusing Congressional funds. After he sat out the 90th Congress, he was overwhelmingly reelected by his Harlem constituents.

In 1969, the Supreme Court ruled that Powell's exclusion from the 90th Congress was unconstitutional. Even though he regained his seat, he lost all seniority and was not restored to his chairmanship. Two years later he was defeated by fellow Democrat Charles Rangel. Powell died in Miami on April 4, 1972. His funeral in Harlem was attended by his former wives, his sons and at least 100,000 mourners.

## Notable Honors and Awards

In addition to being a clergyman, newspaper columnist and politician, Adam Clayton Powell, Jr., was the author of several books. These include *Keep the Faith, Baby!*, published in 1967 and his autobiography, *Adam by Adam*, published in 1971.

He was a delegate to the Parliamentary World Conference in London, England, in 1951-1952 and to the International Labor Organization Conference in Geneva, Switzerland, in 1961. His numerous awards included honorary degrees from Shaw University in 1938 and Virginia Union University in 1947. He was proudest of the Knight of the Golden Cross Medal presented to him in 1954 by Emperor Haile Selassie of Ethiopia for his relief work on behalf of that African nation.

Adam Clayton Powell's life and legislative efforts were dedicated to his uppermost concern—the complete equality of African Americans--for which he earned the title of "Mr. Civil Rights." The controversy that always surrounded him has not detracted from his importance. No less an authority than Dr. Martin Luther King acknowledged Powell's historic role: "For many years you have been a militant champion of justice, not only as a Congressman from Harlem, but necessarily as a spokesman for disenfranchised millions in the South."

(Library of Congress)

*Members of the Black Panther Party confront Powell outside the Education and Labor Committee Room.*

### For Further Reading:

William L. Clay, *Just Permanent Interests: Black Americans in Congress, 1870-1992*, (1993).

Charles V. Hamilton, *Adam Clayton Powell, Jr.: The Political Biography of an American Dilemma*, (1991).

Wil Haygood, *King of the Cats: The Life and Times of Adam Clayton Powell*, (1993).

Adam Clayton Powell, Jr., *Adam By Adam: The Autobiography of Adam Clayton Powell, Jr.*, (1971).

\_\_\_\_\_, *Keep The Faith, Baby!*, (1967).

\_\_\_\_\_, *Marching Blacks: An Interpretive History of the Rise of the Black Common Man*, (1945).

# Harold Washington

*(April 15, 1922-November 25, 1987)*
*Democrat-Illinois (First District)*
*97th-98th Congresses (1981-1983)*

(Moorland-Spingarn Research Center, Howard University)

*Congressman Harold Washington.*

## Symbol of Black Urban Leadership

Harold Washington was born to politics. His service in the Congress of the United States was a brief interlude between his involvement in the politics of the Illinois Legislature and the politics of his hometown of Chicago. The activities during his short tenure in Congress reflected his core concerns—urban policy and protecting voting rights legislation. His efforts in both areas made a difference.

## Background and Political Heritage

Harold Washington was born in Chicago, Illinois, on April 15, 1922, the fourth child of Roy L. Washington and his wife, Bertha Jones Washington. His father was a part-time Methodist minister, a lawyer and a Democratic precinct captain on Chicago's predominantly black South Side at a time when most local residents were Republicans. His mother was a refined, strong-willed woman who read poetry to her children and encouraged them in the arts.

After his parents divorced in 1928, Washington lived with his father. There was no doubt that he was his father's favorite of the four children. The warm relationship between father and son centered around politics. Washington grew up among Chicago's black political elite. William Dawson, who represented Chicago in Congress from 1943 to 1970, and other Democratic leaders were occasional guests in his home. He knew the names of mayors, aldermen and many party officers before he reached his teens. As a boy, he tagged along with his father to political rallies. By fourteen, he helped his father in the precinct, ran errands for the Democratic organization and made political contacts that would be useful in the future.

Washington was an excellent student who loved to read. The public library was close to his home and he was introduced to it early in life by friendly and encouraging librarians. He was also a promising athlete who won a city high school championship in the 120-yard high hurdles in 1939. He was also an amateur middleweight boxer. While he was a good student at Du Sable High School, he did not remain long enough to graduate because school ceased to challenge him. Instead he took a job in a meat packing plant. His father's political connections landed him a desk job at the local U.S. Treasury office. While working there, the 19-year old Washington met and married a 17-year-old young woman who lived in the same apartment building. A few months later he was drafted into the Army Air Corps in 1942.

During World War II, Washington was stationed in a segregated engineer unit in the South Pacific, where he saw little action, but which did allow him time to study the 30 Army correspondence courses that earned him a High School General Equivalency Diploma. He reached the rank of first sergeant and received the Marianas Campaign Ribbon. His marriage did not survive long after the war. By the time Harold was 25, the couple had divorced. For the rest of his adult life, he was a bachelor.

After he was honorably discharged in 1946, Washington studied political science and economics at the newly-created Roosevelt University, one of the few fully integrated institutions of higher education in the country at the time. He had lived most of his life in a segregated society, but he thrived in the new environment. Although he was one of a small number of black students, he won the first of many successful elections in his life when he was elected senior class president in 1949. His leadership qualities were perceived by his mostly white colleagues even then.

After receiving a bachelor of arts degree in 1949, Washington enrolled at Northwestern University Law School, which granted him a law degree in 1952. He briefly shared a law practice with his father until the latter's death in 1953. He then took over the law firm and as captain of his father's precinct. Washington's devotion to his father so impressed Richard J. Daley, the legendary Democratic mayor of Chicago, that he saw to it that he served as an assistant city prosecutor from 1954 to 1958, the first African American to hold that post. Subsequently he was named arbitrator for the Illinois Industrial Commission (1960-64).

## The Metcalfe Political Apprenticeship

With his father's encouragement, Washington had become a close ally to Ralph Metcalfe, a popular local Democratic politician and former sports

(Roosevelt University Archives)

*A young Harold Washington addresses a student meeting at Roosevelt University. Also on the podium are (left to right): Harold Ickes, former Secretary of the Interior and a close advisor to Franklin D. Roosevelt; Chicago businessman and philanthropist Marshall Field III; the university's founding president, Edward J. Sparling; and its vice president, Wayne Leys.*

hero who had run second in the 100-meter dash to Jesse Owens, the champion of the 1936 Olympic Games. Metcalfe, a city councilman and leader of the Democratic Party in the Third Ward, hired Washington as ward secretary and charged him with reorganizing the Young Democrats (YD). It was a perfect vehicle in which to learn ward organization from top to bottom. Under his leadership, the organization's numbers grew to several hundred and became the city's largest and best organized. Moreover, Washington treated it as a training ground for those he brought into the club. He taught them all he knew about politics in late night sessions on parliamentary procedure and political strategy. In theory, he was recruiting new blood for Metcalfe; in fact, he had his own agenda.

Washington proved to be a smart, capable source of political wisdom; and by many accounts, he was really Metcalfe's mentor even though he was many years younger. However, Metcalfe was Washington's official sponsor and shield. Metcalfe was shrewd enough to know Washington was growing restless. When the local state representative retired in 1964, Metcalfe encouraged him to run for the seat.

## Pre-Congressional Elective Office

Following Metcalfe's lead, Washington was elected to the Illinois House of Representatives in 1964. He served six terms in the Illinois House (1965-77) and one term in the state Senate (1977-80). He acquired a reputation as an innovative legislator and an eloquent orator. He drafted bills to strengthen the Illinois Fair Employment Practices Commission, to establish a Martin Luther King state holiday, to protect witnesses and to aid poor and elderly consumers. He devoted many years to support for legislation setting aside funds for minority contractors which finally paid off with its passage in 1979.

Washington had an uneasy relationship with the Chicago Democratic organization (the "machine") led by Mayor Daley. He resented having to vote the straight party line as dictated by the machine. What he called "the idiot card" described the print-out sheet that told the representatives how to vote on every bill. He steadily violated it by voting for the Equal Rights Amendment and annual cost-of-living reviews for public aid recipients, and against state aid vouchers for private and parochial schools. He also helped form the first black caucus in the state legislature. But no matter what else he did, Washington always helped turn out the vote in Chicago for the machine.

## Harold Washington in the U.S. Congress

Representing Chicago's South Side in the United States Congress had been Harold Washington's deepest ambition. The United States House of Representatives to which he was elected in 1980 succeeding Metcalfe was a far cry from the state legislature where microphones were turned off in mid-speech and legislative aides cast votes for absent legislators. In Congress, Washington believed he had finally reached his station in life.

Washington began his short career (1981-83) as a Member of the United States House of Representatives at the same time that Ronald Reagan began his tenure as President of the United States. As an urban liberal Democrat, the new Congressman from Chicago was an ardent

*Class president in his senior year, Washington (second from left) and other students talk with visiting British political scientist and leader of the British Labor Party, Harold Laski (far right).*

opponent of social service cuts and increases in military spending which he believed diverted funds from the poor and disadvantaged, especially in the cities.

He was particularly alarmed by the threat to civil rights advances that he perceived might be slowed when the 1965 Voting Rights Act came up for reauthorization. The legislation had guaranteed African-Americans in the South the right to vote and hold political office. This protection was especially important to members of the Congressional Black Caucus (CBC), many of whom would not have been elected without it. The caucus selected Harold Washington to be the floor leader to retain and expand the law.

His selection as the CBC's floor leader was a great honor for a freshman Congressman, but then Washington was not a typical freshman legislator. He came to Congress with all the skills of a veteran lawmaker. His performance was as astute in the cloakroom as it was on the House floor. Bold and articulate, he emerged as a leading figure in the caucus; in fact, several colleagues wanted him to be its next chairman. He was sitting on top of the world. He told friends that he could live out the rest of his days in Congress and die a happy man.

## Convincing Washington to Run for Mayor of Chicago

Washington's Congressional service ended when he was elected mayor of Chicago in 1982. He had run once before, in a special election following the death of Mayor Daley in 1977; but he finished a distant third, garnering only 11 percent of the vote. It was not a pleasant experience. When he was approached in 1982 by some prominent black Chicagoans to run again in the primary, he was very reluctant to give up his fairly secure seat in Congress.

Washington reluctantly agreed to run for mayor only after 100,000 new voters were registered by his supporters. He was disadvantaged in terms of name recognition outside of his district. He lacked campaign funds and he was running for office in what the United State Civil Rights Commission called the most segregated city in the nation.

The televised debates provided the turning point for his candidacy. His charisma and articulation of the issues won over many voters, especially African-American voters who registered and voted in greater numbers than ever before. It was a shock to the Chicago Democratic political machine when Harold Washington won the primary. Normally, such a victory in a lopsided Democratic city is tantamount to victory in the general election. However, the city Democratic machine chose to support the white candidate of the Republican Party, something that had never happened before in Chicago.

There were many politically significant mayoral races throughout the United States in 1982. However, none captivated the headlines like the Chicago race. The national Democratic Party supported Washington by sending several leaders to Chicago to campaign for him. Washington barely won, with less than 53 percent of the vote; but he did win. In the process, he made history as the first African-American mayor of America's third largest city.

## Washington's Performance as Mayor

In spite of opposition by the Democrat-dominated City Council in the first three years of his mayoral term, Harold Washington was finally able to achieve important reforms. The nearly paralyzing "council wars" subsided after a court-ordered special election in which enough of his allies won council seats to give the mayor a 25-25 split. Using his tie-breaking vote, Washington was able to push through a series of far-reaching measures, including a 72-million-dollar property tax increase to balance the city's budget. (He had honestly promised a tax hike during the campaign).

His supporters were justified and his opponents were relieved to see Mayor Washington appoint respected reform-oriented leaders to key positions in his administration. Streets were repaired that had not seen work crews in years. Trash collection was improved by crews paying more regular visits to the city's crazy quilt of ethnic neighborhoods.

The ugly racial antagonisms of 1982 were absent when Washington ran for a second term in 1986. The principal candidates were the same, Washington and Jane Byrne, the candidate of the historically entrenched Democratic machine. Therefore the winner of the Democratic primary likely would win the general elections. But more importantly, politics in Chicago had changed. Washington had established the viability of black leadership as a factor to be respected by both parties.

## A Second, But Short Mandate in City Hall

Washington's second term as mayor was a marked contrast to the first. Bellicose rhetoric gave way to a mellower, more confident style of leadership. Even with only a one-vote majority supporting Washington on the city council, he could pursue his long delayed reform program with vigor.

The mayor was committed to fairness and equality as a standard for all Americans. He believed in opening up the system to those who

(Chicago Historical Society, ICHi-22781)

*Washington was an active and popular mayor of Chicago. He died in 1987 after a tree-planting ceremony much like the ground-breaking ceremony in 1986 pictured in this photograph.*

traditionally had been left out. His administration was open not only to black citizens, but also to Hispanics, Asians, women and the handicapped. He believed in full employment for all men and women seeking work. He believed that reform, and not necessarily political patronage, opened the system to everyone.

One of the most significant struggles for Mayor Washington was reforming the powerful Park District, notorious as a refuge for whites only, headed by a politically appointed superintendent in charge of 500 parks, a 320-million-dollar annual budget and 6,000 employees. Washington's efforts forced the courts to issue a consent decree to equalize resources for parks in all neighborhoods.

Washington was an active, compassionate mayor right up to the end of his life. The morning of November 25, 1987, he had planted a tree at a ground-breaking ceremony for a new housing development. He was working in his office when he suffered a massive heart attack. His death was a real blow to black urban aspirations and to efforts to make Chicago the more livable and tolerant place it ought to be.

In noting the death of Harold Washington, President Ronald Reagan paid homage to his legacy: "He was a dedicated and outspoken leader who guided one of our nation's largest cities through the 1980s. Harold Washington will truly be missed, not only by the people of Chicago but also by many across the country for whom he provided leadership on urban issues."

**For Further Reading:**

William L. Clay, *Just Permanent Interests: Black Americans in Congress, 1870-1992*, (1993).
Florence Hamlish Levinsohn, *Harold Washington: A Political Biography*, (1983).
Gary Rivlin, *Fire on the Prairie: Chicago's Harold Washington and the Politics of Race*, (1992).

# Andrew Jackson Young, Jr.

*(March 12, 1932-)*
*Democrat-Georgia (Fifth District)*
*93d-95th Congresses (1973-1977)*

(Moorland-Spingarn Research Center, Howard University)

*Congressman Andrew Young.*

## The Conciliator

**M**erhaps no member of Congress was more suited for the role of conciliator than Andrew J. Young, Jr. His privileged background, prominence in the civil rights movement and calm demeanor made him a natural candidate to succeed as the first African American elected in this century to Congress from the Deep South. By the time he took the oath of office in the U.S. House of Representatives, much of the harsh rhetoric and overtly discriminatory practices of the institution had ceased. His mere presence symbolized the emergence of African Americans in the New South, increasing racial harmony and America's renewed moral position abroad.

## Childhood and Education

Andrew J. Young, Jr., was born in New Orleans, Louisiana, on March 12, 1932, the son of Andrew J. Young, a prosperous dentist, and Daisy Fuller Young, a schoolteacher. He and younger brother Walt enjoyed a privileged upbringing even in the segregated South.

Young graduated from Gilbert Academy, a private school in New Orleans, at the age of 15 in 1947. He attended Dillard University for one year before he transferred to his father's alma mater, Howard University in Washington, D.C., as a pre-med student. He earned a bachelor of science degree in 1951 at age 19. While he was at Howard, he had some success as a sprinter and seriously considered trying out for the 1952 Olympics until George Rhoden, the great Jamaican world record holder, outran him in the 440-yard dash at Morgan State College in Baltimore.

After his graduation the family attended a summer conference sponsored by the Congregational Church at Lincoln Academy in North Carolina. Young shared a room with a white minister who had taken his wife and child to Africa to serve as a missionary. This young minister's deep faith had a profound impact and made Young think about his own calling to religious service, as he has recounted in his autobiography, *A Way Out of No Way*. While attending the retreat, he found a new sense of self-discovery and understanding that he had not experienced before.

Given the importance of religion to his family, Young's decision to study for the ministry was not surprising. He had a strong upbringing in the Congregational Church; his father was a deacon and sang in the choir. His mother was the superintendent of the Sunday school and church treasurer.

On a six-month trip though the South with the United Christian Youth Movement, Young met Jean Childs while working in rural Marion, Alabama. They were married on June 7, 1954; but in the meantime, Young attended Hartford Theological Seminary in Connecticut where he earned a bachelor's degree in divinity and was ordained in 1955. Young and his wife returned to Marion where he served as pastor, civil rights coordinator and teacher. Later he served as pastor to congregations in Thomasville and Beachton, Georgia.

The National Council of Churches invited Young to work in the Youth Work Division in New York City. He and his wife moved to New York City where he served as associate director from 1957 to 1961. In the meantime, civil rights activities were developing full force in the South and the couple wanted to return to the region.

Dr. Martin Luther King, Jr., asked Young to serve as his top aide in Atlanta in 1961. Young became a part of the diverse team attracted to King's philosophy of nonviolent change. Later Andy was appointed director of the Southern Christian Leadership Conference (SCLC) in 1964. He was a major planner of the SCLC campaign to desegregate Southern cities. After Dr. King's death in 1968, Young served as SCLC executive vice president until 1970.

Convinced that social change would come mainly through political action, Young decided to run for Congress from Georgia's predominantly white Fifth District. He failed in the initial attempt, but built a biracial coalition of enthusiastic volunteers. From 1970 to 1972 he was chairman of the Atlanta Human Relations Commission. He then ran for the same Congressional seat, which had been redistricted to increase the percentage of black voters to nearly 44 percent. He won by garnering 25 percent of the white vote and most of the black vote. In the 1974 and 1976 elections, he was returned to Congress with 72 and 80 percent, respectively, of the total vote. These election figures represented real progress in biracial voting patterns for his district.

## Congressional Career

Young took his seat in Congress in January 1973, a few weeks before his 40th birthday. He and Barbara Jordan entered Congress at the same time, becoming the first African-American Members of the House from the Deep South since the Reconstruction era. Even before entering Congress, Young had helped to draft the language of the Civil Rights Act of 1964 and the Voting Rights Act of 1965.

Young was first assigned to the House Banking and Currency Committee; but with his 1974 reelection, he became the first African American to join the prestigious and powerful Committee on Rules.

Generally, he established a liberal voting record. He rejected cuts in domestic spending for the poor and voted to raise the minimum wage (including domestic workers), to expand the food stamp program, to establish federal day-care assistance, to fund public service jobs, to provide mortgage subsidies for unemployed homeowners and to create a consumer protection agency. He introduced a bill outlining a comprehensive national health care plan during his tenure in Congress. He also supported a simplified voter registration system and the public financing of Congressional elections. As a strong environmentalist, he supported the establishment of federal standards for surface mining and land reclamation.

(Courtesy of Andrew Young)

*House Majority Leader Tip O'Neill (right) looks on as Speaker Carl Albert swears Young into office in 1973.*

*Israel's United Nations Ambassador Chaim Herzog confers with Ambassador Young in March 1977. Young was President of the UN Security Council that month.*

Young's pacifist views—growing out of his religious beliefs—were often reflected in his positions on war and defense spending. As an early opponent of the Vietnam War, he voted to override President Nixon's veto of the War Powers Act limiting executive war-making powers. He opposed more military aid to the South Vietnamese government, but did vote to send humanitarian and evacuation aid after April 1975. He disapproved of funds for the B-1 bomber, antiballistic missiles and nerve gas.

Congressman Young was a bit of a maverick in his political positions at times. He shocked his Congressional Black Caucus colleagues when he supported the nomination of Gerald R. Ford as President Nixon's vice-presidential replacement. He also defended the decision of President Ford to unconditionally pardon former President Nixon.

His somewhat unpredictable behavior emerged again as the earliest African-American supporter of Jimmy Carter's presidential candidacy in 1976. Young had met Carter when the later ran for governor of Georgia. He concluded that Carter was the best candidate to carry the South and thereby insure the Democratic Party's victory. He mobilized a massive registration drive in inner cities around the country. Those votes provided the margin of Carter's victory over Gerald Ford in the election. It was probably inevitable that Andy would be offered a position in the Carter administration as a result of his efforts; but Young had won his own reelection and was very comfortable serving in Congress.

Soon after the election, the President-elect sent Congressman Young to meet with African leaders in Lesotho. Carter was impressed with Young's depth of knowledge about the continent. The new President asked Young to join his administration as the American Ambassador to the United Nations. Although flattered, Andy resisted because he was happy serving in Congress. Additionally, the position of UN Ambassador in the President's cabinet had previously been rather insignificant. Many of his Congressional Black Caucus colleagues cautioned against accepting the post. He reconsidered only after President Carter assured him that he would have a significant role in the formulation of foreign policy in general.

The controversial nature of Young's appointment emerged in Senate confirmation hearings when he spoke bluntly about his recommendations to the President on the establishment of immediate diplomatic relations with Vietnam and the repeal of the Byrd amendment. (Named for Sen. Harry F. Byrd, Jr., of Virginia, the amendment exempted the United States from participation in United Nations economic sanctions against Rhodesia's white government because the United States imported most of its chrome from that country.) The repeal of the amendment would put the United States in compliance as a member state of the United Nations as well as signal to the world its renewed support for racial democracy in Rhodesia (now Zimbabwe) and South Africa. Young was confirmed by the Senate and soon thereafter the Byrd amendment was repealed.

## The Ambassador to the United Nations

On January 29, 1977, Andrew Young resigned from Congress to become the United States Permanent Representative to the United Nations. He presented his credentials to Secretary General Kurt Waldheim two days later. His well-publicized appointment gained praise for the United States in naming a black citizen to represent it before the principal world forum.